Spectrality and Survivance

Critical Perspectives on Theory, Culture and Politics

This interdisciplinary series was developed in partnership with the Centre for Critical and Cultural Theory at the School of English, Communication and Philosophy, Cardiff University. The series focuses on innovative research produced at the interface between critical theory and cultural studies.

Series editors: Glenn Jordan, Cardiff University; Laurent Milesi, Cardiff University; Radhika Mohanram, Cardiff University; Chris Müller, Macquarie University; Chris Weedon, Cardiff University

Titles in the series:

Spectrality and Survivance

Living the Anthropocene

Marija Grech

ROWMAN & LITTLEFIELD
Lanham • Boulder • New York • London

Published by Rowman & Littlefield
An imprint of The Rowman & Littlefield Publishing Group, Inc.
4501 Forbes Boulevard, Suite 200, Lanham, Maryland 20706
www.rowman.com

86-90 Paul Street, London EC2A 4NE

British Library Cataloguing in Publication Information Available

Library of Congress Cataloging-in-Publication Data

Names: Grech, Marija, 1983- author.
Title: Spectrality and survivance : living the anthropocene / Marija Grech.
Description: Lanham : Rowman & Littlefield, [2022] | Series: Critical perspectives on
    theory, culture, and politics | Includes bibliographical references and index.
Identifiers: LCCN 2022005684 (print) | LCCN 2022005685 (ebook) | ISBN
    9781786614155 (cloth) | ISBN 9781786614162 (paperback) | ISBN
    9781786614179 (epub)
Subjects: LCSH: Philosophical anthropology. | Human beings—Extinction. | Human
    beings—Forecasting.
Classification: LCC BD450 .G683555 2022 (print) | LCC BD450 (ebook) | DDC
    128—dc23/eng/20220404
LC record available at https://lccn.loc.gov/2022005684
LC ebook record available at https://lccn.loc.gov/2022005685

Contents

Acknowledgments

This book would not have been possible without the love, support and encouragement of my parents, Mary Grech and Leonard Grech. To them I owe my deepest gratitude.

I would like to thank Ivan Callus for being such a great mentor, friend and colleague for so many years, and Christopher John Müller for his strength, generosity and kindness. To James Corby and the rest of the English Department at the University of Malta: thank you for providing me with an academic home and a space in which to discuss the future of all that we hold dear. I would also like to thank fellow members of the Critical Posthumanism Network—Stefan Herbrechter, Manuela Rossini and Megen de Bruin-Molé—for being such great colleagues and collaborators.

I am grateful to Chris Weedon for her friendship and guidance, to Vicki Kirby for her work and feedback on my manuscript and to Laurent Milesi and Radhika Mohanram for their support. Thanks are also due to the University of New South Wales's (UNSW Sydney) School of Humanities and Languages for providing me with a three-year visiting research fellowship and a place to work while in Sydney and to the members of UNSW's Environmental Humanities research group for their feedback on some of the earlier versions of these chapters. I am also deeply grateful to Shirley Müller and Urs Müller for reading through my manuscript and helping me with some of the finer points of the scientific research I cite. Any errors or misunderstandings are my own.

To my wider friends and family—including Alison Vassallo, Nicola Mangani, Nicole Bugeja, Siriol McAvoy, Catherine Paula Han, Jernej Markelj, Anna Catania, Anthony Catania, Nina Catania and Michael Catania—thank you for helping me get through what has been a difficult, and at times impossible, couple of years.

~

Introduction

Spectral Present, Specular Futures

Writing in the second half of the 20th century, the German philosopher Günther Anders diagnoses a 'blindness' and a 'muteness' towards the 'apocalypse'—an inability to *see*, to *imagine*, to *feel* and to *speak* about the catastrophes that humankind has created. 'What exceeds our imagination,' Anders explains, 'also exceeds our language. We cannot put it into words, it is "unspeakable."'[1] Here, now, possibly at the end of the world, we may not have the words we need to think and talk about the end. While for Anders it was the possibility of nuclear annihilation that created this incomprehensible 'monstrousness,'[2] the climate and environmental crises of today pose similar challenges. As several commentators have argued, Anders's writings anticipate many of the realities faced by 21st-century Western societies and their continued inability to address what they already know to be true about the world.[3] Although we now inhabit what Srećko Horvat describes as 'post-apocalyptic times'—a time in which the end has already been revealed to us,[4] and, in some cases, has already been lived[5]—many of us remain unable to grasp the true extent of the coming catastrophe.[6]

Popular culture may abound with fictional and non-fictional imaginings of possible apocalyptic and post-apocalyptic scenarios, but many of these remain mere *projections of our incapacity to see*; they hide our inability to engage with that which lies beyond the world as we know it. Joanna Zylinska argues that while apocalyptic images purport to present us with visions of a supposed end, they also obfuscate what is truly at stake in thinking the climate crisis: 'they hide the fact that soon *there will be nothing to see*—and no one to see it.'[7]

This is the unrepresentable truth that Anders calls upon us to open our eyes to and create a language for: the unmitigated and unmediated finality that we are bringing about. After the end of the world, Anders tells us, there will be no possibility of any human vision, no form of human imagination, thought or representation, no sights, no sounds, no language and no knowledge that human beings could access, because there will indeed be no human beings left to access them.[8]

Anders's philosophy calls on us to imagine the unimaginable, to speak the unspeakable, to try to represent that which, by definition, must remain un-representable. It is only by imagining the end of the world and the end of the human species within it, Anders's writings seem to suggest, that we might be able to generate the resolve needed to prevent the climate catastrophe that looms ahead. Taking his lead from Anders, Horvat argues that such thinking would require us to 'go beyond the threshold of what humans can compre-hend,' to 'go beyond history' because 'even if the planet were to continue to exist [after the end of the human species], there would be no more history.'[9] Horvat here echoes comments by the historian Dipesh Chakrabarty, who argues that the climate crisis places the 'future beyond the grasp of historical sensibility' and that it is precisely this 'beyond' that must be imagined and engaged with if we are to collectively address the crises that confront us.[10] David Wood makes a similar point, noting that what is needed in the present is an engagement with the idea of a deep past and a deep future—a depth of time that is so radically outside of human understandings of the world that it remains ungraspable and radically unthinkable, while still needing to be thought.[11] For Wood, the impossible necessity of such thought 'offers grounds for a certain hope.' 'Knowing the show would cease shortly after we died,' he explains, 'would change the meaning we could give to our own lives,' and it could influence the way that we approach our future.[12] It is only by confronting the future absence of the human and the unimaginable depth of time that exists outside of human history and consciousness, these authors suggest, that we might begin to transform the way we think about the world and behave within it.

But if what we need is a true transformation of human thought and action—a radical reshaping of our understanding of the worlds of the pres-ent and the future—then confronting the possibility of a complete absence of human beings upon this earth is not nearly enough. In what follows I argue that apart from trying to imagine the end of the world and the end of all human life, we must also be able to imagine and bring about *an end to human ways of thinking about the world*; we must be able to find a language with which to think and talk about the present and the future that does not privilege the human above all else and does not structure itself around the possible presence or absence of human life upon this planet. The challenge that we face is not merely that of imagining an earth without the human but of conceptualising the earth and our place within it in ways that do not continue to repeat and reproduce the very same anthropocentric values and assumptions that have created the crises we seek to overcome. What follows is one attempt to do this: an attempt to find non-anthropocentric ways of conceptualising the present and the future and of thinking the complex relations that exist between and amongst human beings, other lifeforms and other forms of earthly matter.

The Spectrality of the Present

We live in spectral times—a time in which time itself feels somehow displaced. The present is, to quote Jacques Derrida's paraphrasing of Hamlet, 'a disjointed or disadjusted now,'[13] a now that often seems beside itself, encountered from the outside, blurred and double-visioned. This is an age that is simultaneously both *before* and *after*: it is situated *before* the global environmental catastrophe that we know will soon take place, but also *after* most of the devastating environmental destruction that will have brought about this end. For Jean-Pierre Dupuy, this recalls what Anders described in his writings on the nuclear apocalypse as a time of 'respite'—a time before 'The End of Time' in which the principal mode of being is that of 'not yet being non-existing' or 'not quite yet being non-existing.'[14] As Dupuy puts it, 'we are now living under a suspended sentence, as it were, a stay of execution,'[15] one that has arisen out of the collective acts of self-destruction that we have 'engraved' into our future and 'frozen into fate.'[16] Aware of our own imminent end and the end of the world around us, we live and experience the present as a spectre of itself—we live in a time that is defined by the anticipatory knowledge of its own end and that is haunted by the future memory of itself as past.

Recalling the early months of 2020, when most of the world watched and waited with bated breath as Chinese cities locked down in an attempt to contain what would soon turn into a raging global pandemic, Horvat notes that 'the majority of the world's population was still living in a present that was already past, while China was already in the future.'[17] Those weeks and months felt like final days—like the last few moments before everything would change, or, perhaps, the last few moments in which everything *had already changed*, even though this change was yet to be felt. This temporal displacement was to become one of the most distressing and disarming aspects of pandemic life,[18] but it was already ripe in our collective cultural consciousness well before the pandemic ever took hold. Indeed, for Horvat, the pandemic served as an 'apocalyptic x-ray,' drawing attention to the much wider catastrophes of our time and highlighting how our daily lives have always already been dominated by a sense of impending doom.[19] Karen Barad describes how in 'these troubling times' of environmental destruction and an ongoing nuclear threat, 'the urgency to trouble time, to shake it to its core' has become 'something so tangible, so visceral, that it can be felt in our individual and collective bodies.'[20] For Barad, time has been 'synchronised to a future of No Future,' and the present is 'caught in a pose of holding its breath' before 'the apocalypse-to-come.'[21] We find ourselves 'fixed and fixated on the event horizon of total annihilation' while knowing that this end has effectively already occurred: it has already been set in motion by the actions and inactions of the past, and it has, more literally, already taken place for so many people around the world who have already experienced the aftermath and the effects of nuclear and climate catastrophes.[22]

Anders first identified this temporal spectrality in the second half of the 20th century when he observed that 'at any given moment we have the power to transform any given place on our planet, and even our planet itself into a Hiroshima.'[23] As Joseph Masco explains in his own discussions of the US nuclear complex and the Cold War imaginary, with the creation of the nuclear bomb the world was catapulted into a space of 'temporal ellipsis' in which 'the missiles may have always already been launched' and the end of the world may have effectively already occurred.[24] Before any actual, physical detonation, 'nuclear technologies explode[d] [. . .] experiences of time,'[25] creating an uncanny sense of spectrality that continues to be felt till this day. Indeed, in the 21st century, the threats of climate change and environmental destruction echo and add to this ongoing nuclear threat. As Horvat puts it, 'the end of the "ends of the world" [. . .] is even more likely [today] than in the times when Anders was writing,' and the world has continued to exist in the space of a 'post-apocalyptic present in which our only horizon is the "naked Apocalypse"—or extinction.'[26]

The experience of living 'after the Apocalypse,' to use Horvat's Andersarian phrase, manifests itself most prominently in a widespread tendency in contemporary Western culture to view the present as an already-past, to perceive it as 'already a memory' of itself viewed from the future.[27] Reflecting on the sense of apocalyptic doom that appears to pervade our daily lives, the writer Mark O'Connell describes a certain *telescoping* of time: a transporting of the gaze of the present into a future from which it can look back at itself as past.[28] O'Connell reflects on how the 'quickening shadow' of apocalypse has come to colour every moment of the present as if it were 'a flashback sequence in the first act of a postapocalyptic movie [. . .] right before the events of the main timeline kicked in.'[29] This sensation of temporal spectrality is most clearly felt by O'Connell on a visit to the 'postapocalyptic wasteland' of Chernobyl, where he reflects on 'what the end of the world might look like.'[30] As he roams through the abandoned homes, schools and shops of neighbouring Pripyat, O'Connell is aware of the 'strangeness' of his presence as 'a man from the outside, from the postapocalyptic future' gazing upon the 'artefact[s] of a collapsed civilization.'[31] Within these leftover relics of 'an abandoned past,' O'Connell discovers 'an immersive simulation of the future, an image of what will come in our wake.'[32] Consequently, O'Connell internalises this telescopic gaze, looking back at his *own* world as a similar kind of past, and he reflects on how the world is haunted by *the spectre of what will have been*, as the present comes to constitute a trace of what once was in a future that is not yet.[33]

The telescopic gaze that O'Connell adopts in his musings on Chernobyl and in his experience of daily life exemplifies what I will refer to in what follows as the *future-retro-vision* of our times: a vision of the present that is haunted by the future memory of itself as past. My discussion is anchored in what is arguably the most prominent manifestation of this gesture of future-retrospectivity in contemporary thought: the notion of the Anthropocene. Since the early 2000s, this term has been used to refer to the way in which anthropogenic changes to earth systems have, over the past few centuries and most significantly over the last few decades, left an indelible mark in the earth's strata, and it has been proposed as a way of formally identifying the existence of a new geological epoch characterised by the lasting impact of human beings upon the planet. The notion of the Anthropocene is predicated on the assumption that traces of human activity will remain readable in the rock, allowing future geologists and stratigraphers to detect and correctly identify the mark of human presence many hundreds of thousands, or even millions, of years from now. While the naming of eons, eras and epochs by geologists and stratigraphers typically relies on a *retrospective* study of the earth's history that looks back into the deep past, examining how the marks of early geological events were recorded in the strata, in their efforts to identify and name the *current* geological epoch as that of the Anthropocene, proponents of this term seek to show how *present-day* anthropogenic events will be stratigraphically recorded as traces of the past *in the future*. Rather than merely providing a *retrospective* study of the history of the earth, these scientists must engage in a speculative and anticipatory *future-retrospective* reading of the strata that seeks to pre-emptively recognise *what will have been*.

As Claire Colebrook notes, 'the positing of the anthropocene era relies on looking at our own world and imagining it as it will be when it has become the past.'[34] Indeed, the Anthropocene paradigm is structured by a gesture of future-retro-vision in which the present functions as the spectral past of a speculative future. There are two sides to this anthropocenic gaze and its spectral haunting of the present: on the one hand, as I have already begun to outline, the present feels *absent* to itself, not fully present, dislodged and displaced, interrupted and disrupted by the prospect of its own end. If the present functions as a future past, then it cannot be truly *present*—it will always be haunted by the possibility of its own future absence and by the knowledge of its own potential radical non-existence. But while the spectral temporality of the Anthropocene brings this absence into view, inviting us to confront the possibility of our own end and the end of the world as a whole, it simultaneously also posits the *continued existence* of the world of the present in the future. While it makes the present absent to itself through the spectrality of its gaze, the future-retro-vision of the Anthropocene remains predicated on the possibility of a human presence that *continues to haunt the future*—it posits an absence that *remains present* as a spectral trace of itself, lingering on in the space of its own supposed nothingness.

My analysis in what follows is rooted in a critique of this complex inter-play of presence and absence. I seek to show how the future-retrospectivity of the Anthropocene is structured by an anthropocentric logic that must be overcome if we are to confront the problems that we face today. While the naming of the current geological epoch as the age of the human (or *anthropos*) might appear to call out human beings for the damage they have wrought upon the earth, this term inadvertently also commemorates and glorifies the exceptional power that human beings now appear to have.[35] As many commentators have argued, the notion of the Anthropocene may be said to constitute the height of anthropocentrism because it posits human beings as central to the workings of the earth in a way that 'rival[s] the great forces of nature,'[36] and it anoints them as saviours and redeemers of the planet, confirming their exceptional status upon it.[37] This anthropocentrism, I argue, is rooted in future-retrospective gestures that appear to *defamiliarise* the present, inviting us to confront the possibility of our own demise and the non-existence of the world as we know it, but that simultaneously also continue to reassert the *presence* of the human upon the earth in a way that undermines the possibility of thinking any true human absence. This anthro-pocentrism makes itself felt in numerous discourses and practices of our time in which the attempt to conceptualise and construct new paths for the future is undercut by an underlying anthropocenic logic that prohibits the possibility of any true change. This book critiques and analyses the functioning and implications of this logic and explores alternative ways of thinking the world of the present and its relation to the future.

The present is and always has been spectral. Jacques Derrida argues as much in *Specters of Marx*, where he comments on what he calls the 'disjoin-ture in the very presence of the present' and the 'non-contemporaneity of present time with itself.'[38] As he explains in the essay "Différance," every moment is always divided from itself; it is always constituted out of a rela-tion to the past, to the future and to 'what it is not.' Derrida notes that 'an interval must separate the present from what it is not in order for the present to be itself, but this interval that constitutes it as present must, by the same token, divide the present in and of itself.'[39] No moment can ever be fully present to itself, as indicated by our very own experience of time in which every moment bleeds into another, always being constituted by that which has just passed and that which is not yet. This non-contemporaneity of the present with itself might be said to be more acutely felt nowadays, in our own anthropocenic age, when we are confronted by the knowledge that our days are numbered. Indeed, in the future-retrospectivity of the Anthropocene, we view ourselves and the world around us as if everything were, as Derrida says of Robinson Crusoe, 'already dead [. . .] already past,' 'already memory and melancholy, or nostalgia.'[40] The present is fractured, reflected back to us from a position of future anteriority. But, as I show in what follows, the anthropo-centric nature of our thought means that these contemporary intimations of our own spectrality are always mediated by a continued sense of presence— by a '*phantasm* of survival,' to quote Michael Naas[41]—that continues to as-sert and affirm the importance and significance of the human, even while it appears to anticipate its demise. Even when we attempt to think the end of the human, even when we are compelled to look back at ourselves from a future in which we supposedly do not exist, our thought remains dominated by the possible presence and absence of the human upon the earth in the present and the future.

Beyond the non-presence of every temporal moment to itself, however— beyond, that is, the spectral understanding of the present as temporally fractured—everything *else* that we think of as a form of presence or as being present is also always already immanently spectral, always divided, always constituted out of otherness. For Derrida, 'everything that is thought on the basis of the present' is constructed out of a relation 'to something other than itself.'[42] Who and what we are as human subjects and biological organisms, and who and what every*one* and every*thing* else is, is spectral because there can be no such thing as unmediated presence. This means, as Barad tells us, that spectral 'haunting' should not simply be understood as 'one or another form of subjective human experience—the epistemological revivications of the past, a recollection through which the past makes itself subjectively present'—or even, one might add here, through which the present appears as a future-past. 'Hauntings,' Barad explains, 'are *material*,' they are the 'ontological re-memberings' of all material existence.[43] Every form of existence, whether living or not, is haunted by the otherness and the difference that constitutes it. This is, I argue, how the apparent spectrality of the present should be approached and interpreted. If we are to truly examine the spectrality of the Anthropocene, then we cannot merely occupy ourselves with speculations over the relative presence or absence of human beings upon this earth, or even the possible presence or absence of *life* more generally. Our understanding of spectrality must push beyond the limitations of these oppositions, concepts and boundaries and seek to discover the inherent non-simultaneity of presence in the entanglement of different forms of life and matter. This might help us, in the words of Derrida, to 'learn to live finally'[44]—or perhaps even 'learn to die'[45]—in ways that do not merely valorise our *own* lives (as individual subjects and as human beings) or even *life* itself but that also grant value and significance to other forms of matter upon this earth.

Future-Retro-Visions

The gesture of future-retrospectivity that I have isolated above is often mobilised as a conceptual tool to help people better understand the environmental problems of our age and address the need for urgent change. Cultural anthropologist Vincent Ialenti notes that 'our most crucial Anthropocene task' is to better understand 'futures near and deep'—to better 'reckon' with the idea of deep time in a way that can allow us to 'grasp the scale of the Earth's ecological death spiral' and find 'escape routes for breaking out of our shortsighted mental strictures.'[46] E. Ann Kaplan likewise argues that we must be able to 'foresee' the destruction of the future—to feel the 'pre-traumatic stress' of the coming environmental catastrophe—if we are to try to prevent it,[47] while Rob Nixon places his faith in what he terms the 'spirit of anticipatory memory' that dominates the Anthropocene,[48] arguing that such gestures can draw attention to the widespread destruction being wrought upon the planet and shake us out of our paralysing inertia.

Nixon discusses how the imagining of 'anticipatory histories'—specular imaginings of the future in which the present appears as an apocalyptic past—can 'encourage us to break out of our temporal silos and [. . .] face the challenges that shadow the path ahead.'[49] 'Nonfictional forays into the future,' Nixon explains, can 'warn us of coming disasters' and push 'us to take action'; they can 'catalyze the change we need' to 'help avert the most ravaging outcomes' of a climate disaster. Appeals by activists such as Greta Thunberg to imagine a future world in which our descendants look back at us in bafflement and anger, wondering why no one did anything 'when there was still time to act,'[50] or texts such as Naomi Oreskes and Erik Conway's *The Collapse of Western Civilization* (2014) that transport readers to the future in order to consider what might remain of the present world after a catastrophic collapse, are intended to combat our 'denial and self-deception,'[51] providing us with a vision of the future that we must, as Kaplan puts it, 'at all costs, avoid.'[52]

These gestures may be said to function as examples of what the theorist Jean-Pierre Dupuy calls 'enlightened doomsaying': they provide readers with a dystopian vision of a possible future in the hopes that this future will never come into being.[53] Reflecting on the obstacles that contemporary Western societies must overcome in order to avert a climate catastrophe, Dupuy explains that one of the greatest hurdles is 'the impossibility of believing that the worst is going to occur.'[54] The 'antidote' to this inability to believe that which we already know to be true about the future[55]—or, as Anders puts it, the inability to *visualise, imagine, feel* and *express* the extent of our impact on the world[56]—is encapsulated for Dupuy in future-retrospective gestures that pre-emptively proclaim the end of the world in order to prevent it from taking place. 'The idea,' Dupuy tells us, 'is to project oneself into the future and look back at our present,'[57] to transport oneself 'into the time following the catastrophe, conceiving of the event in the future perfect tense' so as to 'heighten public awareness and bring about concerted action so that the catastrophe does not occur.'[58] Either implicitly or explicitly, these texts and many others operate under the assumption—or at least in the hope—that the 'hindsight' they provide will inspire 'foresight' and that this might rally audiences into desiring and bringing about change.[59]

However, as I show in what follows, this desire to create the conditions for change in the present and the future is often fundamentally undermined by the very logic of future-retro-vision that these discourses adopt. In many of its manifestations, the attempt to look back at the present from the position of an imagined future does not so much create the possibility for radical change as foreclose it. The speculative and specular device of future-retro-vision does not open our eyes to something outside of ourselves that we cannot see; instead, it holds up a mirror for us to continue to see ourselves in. The very act of future-retrospection through which the present is projected onto a supposedly unknown and unknowable future transforms this future into a reflection of the present, a reflection that serves to assert and affirm the significance and centrality of human presence upon the earth instead of radically challenging it. Rather than opening up the possibility of a *different* future, this gaze reflects the present *back at itself*, reproducing and replicating it in this very reflection. Such a specular and circular logic co-opts both our understanding of the present and our visions for the future, restricting our ability to view the world differently and ensuring that the same anthropocentric values and assumptions that structure the present will be projected into the futures that we create. In the place of change, this logic offers stasis, in the place of difference, the repetition of the self-same.

A closer look at the notion of enlightened doomsaying as exemplified in the work of Günther Anders can help demonstrate why this is the case. Jean-Pierre Dupuy uses a retelling of the biblical story of Noah by Anders to show how the prophesising of future catastrophes can help combat public denial and resistance to something like the truth of global warming.[60] In Anders's rendition of this biblical tale,[61] Noah is cast in the role of enlightened doomsayer. Fearful of the catastrophic flood that he knows is imminent, and frustrated by the unwillingness of his peers to take heed of his repeated warnings, Noah puts on an elaborate show of grieving for the future, shocking his fellow townsfolk by going into mourning and performing prayers for those that 'will have died' from the flood 'tomorrow.' Pushing his listeners to confront the possibility of their own imminent demise, Noah adopts and enacts the future perfect tense that should by now be amply familiar to us: 'The day after tomorrow,' he tells the crowd that gathers around him, 'the flood *will have been* something that happened'; 'the day after tomorrow [. . .] *we will have died*.'[62] Noah's efforts work. Before too long there is a knock at the door: 'Let me help build [the ark]—so [this future] becomes untrue.' The townsfolk are shaken into action by Noah's words and his accompanying performance, and Anders's tale closes, if not with a happy ending, then at least with the knowledge that the unthinkable future that Noah had anticipated was averted: the ark was built and Noah and his progeny were able to survive and repopulate the earth.

At first glance, Noah's enlightened doomsaying seems to perfectly encapsulate the kinds of future-retrospective gestures I am analysing here, and the public response to Noah's words appears to fulfil Rob Nixon's hopes for the texts he surveys—that the imagining of a world that 'will have been' will avert the impending climate catastrophe and result in much-needed change.[63] But, crucially, while the future-retrospective gestures of these texts project themselves into a future from which the present can be looked back at as that which *will have been*, what Noah pushes his fellow townsfolk to confront is quite the opposite: the possibility of a future in which the world of the present 'will *never* have been.'[64] In Anders's retelling of this biblical tale, Noah's mourning for tomorrow must occur *today*, because 'tomorrow when the flood comes it will be too late to remember or to mourn. There will be no one left to mourn us, no one who could hold our memory.' While the gesture of future retrospectivity projects itself into a future world that is inhabited by traces and memories of the present, Anders's work presents readers with a fundamentally *different* kind of future: one that is entirely devoid of any such memory or trace, one in which the present world will, for all intents and purposes, *never* have existed because there will be nothing and nobody left to remember it.[65]

Anders's use of the future perfect does not invite the reader to look back at the present as a *future past*; it pushes one to consider how, in the future, *there may be no such past*. As Anders explains elsewhere, what must be confronted today is a future in which 'the past will not even have been the past,' because there will be no memory and no mourning, nothing left to recognise or remember it.[66] It is the threat of complete oblivion that drives Noah's townsfolk to action: they are not compelled to change their behaviour by some retrospective vision of themselves seen from the future but by the realisation that there might be no such future for them to look back at themselves from, even if only speculatively. What Anders mobilises in his work, therefore, is not the possible logic of a future-retro-vision but precisely the *impossibility* of any such vision. The texts that Nixon surveys might at first glance seem to participate in a similar kind of rhetoric to that used by Anders, employing the future perfect in an attempt to bring about change. But in these works, the gestures of future-retrospectivity establish and affirm the continued *presence* of the human, representing its continued *survival* in the future rather than placing the very possibility of any kind of future and any kind of survival into doubt. In their speculative imaginings, these anticipatory histories identify, affirm and establish a continued human *presence* (even in futures that are supposed to be devoid of any form of human life), and their attempts to warn the present about the future—to present readers with a vision of a dystopian world that will shake them out of their stupor—is covertly undermined and eroded by the implicit promise of survival. The continued representation of the human, or even of the *idea* of the human, persisting intact in its travels through time, being affirmed and even vindicated in the ultimate survival of its memory, dampens the urgency of any perceived threat by transforming the foretelling of doom into an effective immortalisation of the human.

A clear example of this immortalising glance can be found in Alan Weisman's speculative imagining of a supposedly post- or inhuman future in *The World Without Us* (2007). In this popular work of non-fiction, referred to by Dipesh Chakrabarty as a 'brilliant' engagement with the 'deep contradiction and confusion' of our spectral times,[67] readers and viewers are invited to 'look around [. . .], at today's world' so as to consider what might remain of it in a post-human future—to consider how 'some faint, enduring mark [. . .]; some lasting glow, or echo, of Earthly humanity; some interplanetary sign that once we were here' might survive in our wake.[68] Weisman's whole thought experiment is predicated on the possibility of a future world that is completely devoid of any human presence. But this premise is paradoxically undercut by the very gaze of the text itself that projects itself into the future to look back at the present as past. Chakrabarty perceives Weisman's text as an example of how the current climate crisis supposedly 'disconnects the future from the past by putting such a future beyond the grasp of historical sensibility.'[69] But the text can only do so by projecting *itself* and its *readers* into this future, reinstating the historical connection that it supposedly annuls. As Chakrabarty himself notes, 'we have to insert ourselves into a future "without us" in order to be able to visualize it.'[70] One way in which Weisman does this is by mobilising a classic trope of speculative non-fiction—the trope of the 'far-distant future reader' that has its roots in 18th-century geology[71]— inviting us to imagine future 'tourists,' 'geologists,' 'archaeologists' and 'visiting alien scientists' discovering and recognising traces of a human past upon the earth.[72] This trope establishes a continued presence for the human in this supposedly inhuman world, as do the actual material traces and relics of the present-made-past that Weisman imagines 'defend[ing] humanity's memory,' bearing 'witness to the fact that, once, we were here.'[73] Together with the anthropomorphic *eye/I* that lingers on, recognising and reinstating the continuity of the human in this supposedly post-human future, the imagined observable relics that Weisman describes as marks of a past human presence testify to the continued survival of the human upon this earth, even in its own supposed absence.

A similar gaze permeates the 2010 documentary film by Michael Madsen *Into Eternity: A Film for the Future*, which takes as its subject the Onkalo nuclear waste repository currently under construction in Finland.[74] As indicated by its subtitle, the film posits itself as a message to the future, addressing itself to a possible future audience in a purported attempt to engage with an unknown and unknowable world hundreds of thousands of years from now. But contrary to what its title suggests, this film is not really a 'film for the future,' and its purpose is not to familiarise future audiences with the present but to defamiliarise the present for the audiences of today. Gazing directly into the camera, Madsen transposes his present-day viewers into the position of a future audience, asking them, '[I]f *you*, sometime far into the future, find this, what would it tell you about us?.' The film goes on to engage in speculative projections and retrospections, inviting its viewers to wander into the space of a supposedly unknown world so as to look back at the present from a vantage point. In so doing, it projects its own voice and its own gaze onto this future, transforming it into a speculative and specular lens through which to view the present. Beyond its rhetorical ploy, the gaze that is mobilised in this film remains that of the audience of *today*, a familiar human gaze that looks back at itself as through a mirror, asserting its continued presence and survival upon the earth. Like Weisman's text, this film illustrates the *specularity* and *circularity* of future-retrospective gestures that project the present onto the future only to then reflect this present back at itself from this supposedly new vantage point. Such texts may appear to engage with a future that is fundamentally different to the present: a world so completely devoid of human presence that it would in essence remain unthinkable,[75] or a future so temporally remote and distant that it would lie, as David Wood puts it, 'beyond our ordinary comprehension.'[76] But underneath the surface, these gestures of future-retro-vision and the worlds they evoke remain mere *reflections of the present*—specular devices that reproduce rather than fundamentally challenge the frameworks and assumptions that underpin our present world.

Decentring the Anthropocene

The implications of this circular and specular logic become highly significant in the context of the Anthropocene. Tom Cohen and Claire Colebrook note that when the notion of the Anthropocene was first conceptualised, it appeared to open up the possibility of a radically non-anthropocentric vision of the world, the possibility of a different understanding of the present that could change the way we approach the future. In its attempts to grapple with a time far beyond our own—a time in which human beings may no longer be present upon the earth—the Anthropocene seemed to promise a new way of thinking that could generate 'viewpoints, framings or intuitions of an inhuman look,' or even refuse 'the inscription of "the" human altogether.'[77] This geological concept promised to defamiliarise the present, inviting us to view the earth through 'another eye entirely.'[78] But the logic of future-retrospectivity that structures this geological paradigm undermines any such possibility. While it might appear to invite 'a proleptic memorial of ecocide from a back-glance that is not anthropoid at all,'[79] in its conceptualisation

of the traces of human activity on the earth as being geologically and stratigraphically readable, the notion of the Anthropocene betrays the possibility
of any such 'ex-anthropic perspective,'[80] reinstating the figure of the human
right at the moment that it appears to cast it aside.[81]

Inherent in the very conceptualisation of the present as a future geological
epoch is the assumption that there will be someone or something left in the
future able to identify, study and classify the past. The notion of the Anthropocene borrows its legitimacy from the speculative space of a *post*-Anthropo-
cene that remains essentially *human* in its conceptualisation. Rather than 'a
destroyer of anthropisms,' what one finds when one delves into the concept
of the Anthropocene is 'a bluff that mutates,' 'a Trojan Horse.'[82] As in Weisman's imagining of a post-human world, or Madsen's supposed address to the
audiences of a distant age, the notion of the Anthropocene projects its very
own anthropomorphic gaze onto the future, populating this remote world
with anthropocentric assumptions about what has meaning and value upon
this earth. This gaze is personified in the figures of future geologists and explorers who are imagined discovering the remains of human civilisation upon
the earth.[83] But even when such tropes are not explicitly invoked, the logic
of future-retro-vision remains integral to the very conceptualisation of the
Anthropocene and its envisioning of the present as a future past.

The anthropocentrism that structures these gestures of future-retrospectivity is inherently problematic. If, as countless scholars have argued, the
environmental degradation of the past centuries and decades is the result
of an incessant privileging of the human over every other form of life and
matter, then any attempt to address the environmental problems of our time
must necessarily also challenge the anthropocentric assumptions that fuel
them. As the use of the alternative term 'Capitalocene' indicates,[84] the effects of environmental destruction witnessed in the Anthropocene are the
result of centuries-long imperialist, capitalist and industrialist expansion in
which particular groups of human beings assigned themselves power and
privilege under the guise of some universal 'human.' The belief in human
exceptionalism has fuelled and legitimised discourses and practices that commodify non-human species, earthly matter and other groups of human beings, transforming them all into resources for capitalist and imperialist use.[85]
As Kathryn Yusoff shows, it is on the violent exploitation and 'extraction' of
'properties and personhood' deemed to be less than human—the exploitation
of 'inhuman' earthly matter, non-human species and dehumanised persons—
that the world of the Anthropocene has been built.[86] If the environmental
and climactic challenges of our time are to be adequately addressed, then it
is precisely this valorising of the 'human' over everything else that must be

confronted and undone. In Eileen Crist and Helen Kopnina's diagnosis, anthropocentrism and the notion of human exceptionalism constitute the 'root
causes [. . .] of the pressing problems of our day,'[87] and it is our reliance on
the deeply entrenched anthropocentric assumptions of Western thought that
must be uprooted if there is to be any hope for the future.

While the notion of the Anthropocene might at first appear to offer the
possibility of a radically different engagement with the earth, opening up
inhuman vistas that disrupt and fragment human frames of reference and
systems of thought, in its reliance on the logic of future-retro-vision, this
geological and cultural paradigm continues to be structured by an anthropocentric framework that transforms any thought of the future into an anthropomorphic projection of the present. The question that confronts us here is
whether there might still be ways of engaging with the notion of the Anthropocene that do not fall back into these anthropocentric structures; ways
of thinking the Anthropocene that resist the draw of its future-retrospective
gaze. The work of Günther Anders and his resistance to the logic of future-
retro-vision appear to offer one possible solution: rather than looking back at
the present as that which *will have been*, one could try to imagine the world as
that which will *never* have been. Instead of reflecting on how human civilisation will be immortalised in the stratigraphic marks and traces that will supposedly remain readable in the earth as signs of a past human presence, one
might choose to engage with the thought of a complete and utter expiration
of humankind that would leave 'no memory in any being, engulfing all existence in darkness.'[88] The ending to Madsen's documentary appears to gesture
towards such a vision.[89] Having presented the site of the Onkalo nuclear
waste repository as a possible future trace or record of human activity on the
earth, and having fashioned itself as a message from the present intended for
the anthropomorphic audiences of a remote future, Madsen's film closes with
a meditation on how the very radiation contained at this site could in the
future extinguish the lives of all those who come across it. In its final lingering shots, Madsen's film takes on an Andersarian tone as it pushes its viewers
to consider how the radioactive traces left behind at Onkalo might *themselves*
be what wipe out any thought or memory of the present, replacing everything
that *will have been* with nothingness, effectively annulling the existence of
any human past and, with it, the possibility of any continued future.

Such thoughts of complete annihilation appear to reverse the logic of
future-retro-vision, presenting us with an absolute absence of any human
world in the place of its surviving presence. But, paradoxically, such conceptualisations of human absence as a complete and utter nothingness also
inadvertently continue to reproduce the same anthropocentric logic that we

must seek to overcome. As Anders himself indicates, the eradication of all human life does not actually amount to *nothingness*—it does not amount to an extinguishing of every other material or biological form of existence on this earth. It is not 'the world as a whole' that will descend into 'nothingness' after all traces of human existence have been wiped out, but '*the world as mankind*'—everything that constitutes a *human world*, the world *for and of the human.*[90] The nothingness that Anders's work confronts us with only constitutes an absolute void if we continue to think about the earth in human terms. But an earth devoid of human life—or even, for that matter, an earth devoid of *all life*—would not be a vacuum in which nothing else is and 'nothing ever was.'[91] The *materiality* of the earth itself would still remain— a materiality that has its own past and that is itself entangled in the many biological and discursive histories of human and non-human lives with and within which it has unfolded. Apart from human life, human presence, human memory and human thought, there are multitudes of *other* material and biological forms of survival and persistence, *other* traces and memories that weave their own trajectories through the past, the present and the future while also being entangled in human systems of meaning and human ways of living. Rather than viewing the present and the future as solely marked by the continued *presence*, or, equally, the absolute *absence* of human beings, we can shift and multiply our perspective to consider how the earth manifests *many other* possible kinds of markings, many other interminglings of presences and absences, both human and non-human, living and non-living, organic and inorganic, discursive, biological and material.

It may be useful here to think of that radioactive waste that continues to live on at the end of Madsen's film even after it may have eradicated every last trace of human or even non-human life. In discourses on the Anthropocene, and indeed in Madsen's documentary, such radioactive remains are generally read as *semiotic* marks, as meaningful traces or representational signs that point back to a human presence upon the earth. And within a human frame of reference—within, for instance, the disciplines of geology and stratigraphy and the discourses of a 21st-century Western cultural imaginary—these material traces *do* indeed function as such geochemical signals: as marks or inscriptions on the earth that can be read and interpreted *by* the human, as signs *of* the human. But the existence of radioactive matter—the materiality of the decaying waste that will be interred at the Onkalo site, for instance, or the geochemical traces of atmospheric radiation from the testing of nuclear weapons in the second half of the 20th century that are being sedimented into the strata of the earth as we speak—do not simply constitute a semiotic mark. Although the lives (or perhaps the 'half-lives') of such radioactive matter are intimately intertwined with the human discursive and material structures and practices that have directed and shaped the creation, use and subsequent disposal of nuclear materials, the continued existence of these geochemical phenomena cannot be reduced to a mere semiotic marker. The many material and geochemical 'marks' that are read and interpreted as human inscriptions upon the earth—as the future remains of the Anthropocene by which the world of the present will be remembered and possibly even mourned—exist, subsist, persist and survive not merely as signs of something past but as *material* entities that live and live on through the many chemical, biological and discursive interactions that constitute them.

Derridean Materialism

An increased awareness of the interconnectedness of human beings with and within other complex living and material phenomena is foundational to the work of many posthumanist and new materialist thinkers. Theorists working in these fields seek to problematise the perceived oppositions between nature and culture, the human and the non-human, the animate and the inanimate, with the aim of fundamentally challenging notions of human exceptionalism and the power structures they entail. Foundational to this undertaking is a desire to find new ways of addressing the environmental problems of our time and to develop new ways of thinking and living, both in the present and for the future. Stacy Alaimo and Susan Heckman argue that 'thinking through the co-constitutive materiality of human corporeality and nonhuman natures offers possibilities for transforming environmentalism itself,'[92] while Diana Coole and Samantha Frost comment on how recent crises 'call upon us to reorient ourselves profoundly in relation to the world, to one another, and to ourselves' by 'think[ing] in new ways about the nature of matter and the matter of nature; about the elements of life, the resilience of the planet, and the distinctiveness of the human.'[93] Resisting the widespread desire to 'address trouble' by orienting oneself toward the future—predicting, preventing or protecting possible future worlds—Donna Haraway argues that what is needed is for us to learn 'to be truly present,' not by foregrounding the presence and priority of individual human identities but by recognising how human beings and their worlds are 'entwined in myriad unfinished configurations of places, times, matters, meanings.'[94] For Karen Barad this means that the very relationship between matter and meaning must be rethought and the distribution of agency across 'nonhuman as well as human forms' accounted for.[95] 'Learning how to intra-act responsibly within and as part of the world means understanding that we are not the only active beings,' Barad argues, while she also cautions that 'this is never justification for deflecting that responsibility onto other entities.' Living responsibly demands a form of accountability that is attentive to the rich complexity of earthly interaction and the way that this complexity has been subsumed under 'existing power asymmetries.'[96]

It is within this rich trajectory of scholarship that this book situates itself. In the chapters that follow, I seek alternative ways of thinking and writing about the Anthropocene that can help reconceptualise our understanding of the present and our expectations about what might constitute a future. My discussions zero in on what is perhaps *the* conceptual cornerstone of this contemporary scientific and cultural paradigm: the idea of an anthropogenic trace or mark upon the earth. Exploring the use of linguistic and textual metaphors in descriptions of such stratigraphic marks—such as the frequently used image of a human 'signature' in the rocks[97]—I question the ways in which certain geochemical phenomena have come to be viewed predominantly as future representational signs of a past human presence, and I argue that such a semiotic understanding of these phenomena should be modulated by a wider consideration of the *materiality* of their existence. Resisting the anthropocentric pull of the specular and speculative logic that lies at the heart of the anthropocenic imaginary, I propose an alternative reading of the concept of the lithic trace—one that does not reduce the geochemical traces in the earth's strata to human semiotic marks but that seeks to examine the complexity of their material existence in their entanglements with other forms of living and non-living, human and non-human matter. Drawing on recent bio- and eco-deconstructive readings of the work of Jacques Derrida, I explore how notions of reading and writing can be expanded and reconceptualised to account for the different geological, chemical and biological inscriptions of matter—inscriptions that do not depend on or require any human linguistic forms of semiotic production or reception. Approaching the Anthropocene from a position that is at once both materialist and Derridean in its leanings and its concerns, I thus seek to develop a thinking of the trace that demonstrates the interconnectedness of human and non-human life and matter in a way that undoes some of the primary assumptions and conceptual structures that underpin the anthropocentric frameworks of the Anthropocene.

The work of Jacques Derrida, with its particular focus on questions of textuality, is often associated with a certain 'neglect of [. . .] material phenomena and processes.'[98] The linguistic or cultural turn in philosophy, as it is often referred to, is mostly understood to constitute a turn *away* from matter, materiality and materialism, one that 'privileges language, discourse, culture, and values' in a radically constructivist framework.⁹⁹ While acknowledging that the work of 20th-century continental philosophers and theorists such as Derrida served to problematise any 'naively representational or naturalistic' approach to matter and 'alert[ed] us to the way power is present in any attempt to map material reality,' Diane Coole and Samantha Frost consider poststructuralist concerns with language and culture as inadequate for a thinking of matter. If we are to 'reopen the issue of matter' and 'give material factors their due in shaping society and circumscribing human prospects,' Coole and Frost argue, then the linguistic turn must itself be turned away from.¹⁰⁰ Similarly, in their introduction to *Material Feminisms*, Stacy Alaimo and Susan Heckman identify 'serious liabilities' in a tradition of continental thought that appears to sideline 'the concept of the real or the material' by contending 'that the real/material is entirely constituted by language.'¹⁰¹ Asserting the importance of a new materialism, Alaimo and Heckman insist on the need to correct what they view as a 'retreat from materiality' in order to allow for a closer engagement with 'lived experience, corporeal practice, and biological substance' within a 'more-than-human world.'¹⁰²

Such objections to poststructuralist theory, and to the linguistic turn often associated with the work of Derrida, are not limited to the field of new materialism. Although, as Martin Hägglund points out, Derrida is not typically mentioned by name in Quentin Meillassoux's speculative realist critique of 'correlationalism,' he is generally understood to be one of its intended targets.¹⁰³ For Meillassoux, all philosophical thought after Kant is based on a fundamental separation between 'thinking and being' that prohibits access to 'the *great outdoors*.'¹⁰⁴ Although so-called correlationist thought might 'insist that consciousness, like language, enjoys an originary connection to a radical exteriority,' it nevertheless remains imprisoned within the very exteriority that it itself sets up.¹⁰⁵ For Meillassoux, the 'outside' posited by a thinker such as Derrida is a 'cloistered outside' that we are *'always-already'* within—an outside that is entirely 'relative to us' because it 'exists only as a correlate of our own existence.' The 'space of exteriority' opened up by poststructuralist theory is 'merely the space of what faces us'; it denies access to any outside that is 'not relative to us' and would exist 'regardless of whether we are thinking it or not.'¹⁰⁶ If we are to escape this imprisonment—'*to get out of ourselves, to grasp the in-itself, to know what is whether we are or not*'¹⁰⁷—then this 'circle of correlation' and its implicit 'species solipsism' must be broken out of.¹⁰⁸ For Meillassoux the challenge that faces contemporary thought is that of casting off the shackles of correlationism so as to 'carve out a path towards the outside itself' and finally engage with the true 'materialism of matter.'¹⁰⁹

As Jonathan Basile notes, it has by now become almost standard practice for new materialist and speculative realist thinkers to denounce deconstruction's supposed misguided concern with 'anthropocentric forms of representation' and to berate its apparent inability to engage with 'being, matter, or things in themselves.'[110] But as Basile outlines, such rebukes are generally predicated on a widespread misunderstanding of Derrida's work that does not take seriously the ways in which this poststructuralist thinker radically reconceptualises notions of writing and textuality, pushing these concepts beyond any merely human, cultural, linguistic or semiotic frame of reference. This is epitomised in the persistent misreading of Derrida's now notorious assertion in *Of Grammatology*: '*il n'y a pas de hors-texte*' ('there is no outside-text' or 'there is nothing outside of the text').[111] This phrase has been understood by many as the ultimate expression of a linguistic constructivism that imprisons human beings in language, prohibiting any engagement with a non-linguistic 'outside.'[112] As Matthias Fritsch, Philippe Lynes and David Wood argue, in such readings, 'references to the outside—the real, materiality, or life itself—are supposedly rendered impossible by linguistic and textual traces that come to take their place,' and Derrida's notion of a 'general text' is understood as referring to 'linguistic and cultural webs of meaning' that 'form the ultimate context, the limit beyond which it would be futile to seek to go.'[113] But the notion of 'general text' as it is used by Derrida does not simply refer to linguistic, cultural and human systems of reference. As Fritsch, Lynes and Wood explain, Derridean textuality encompasses 'human systems of notation as much as prelinguistic, nonanthropological marks or modes of existence,' and it 'precedes oppositions between economy and ecology, thought and nature, or human and animal or vegetal life.'[114] General textuality extends beyond human language, beyond human life and even beyond life itself, pointing to what Pheng Cheah describes as 'the opening up or overflowing of any form of presence such that it becomes part of a limitless weave of forces or an endless process of movement or referral.'[115] As Vicki Kirby puts it, human and non-human life and matter are all '*différant* expressions of a unified field' in which language, life and 'the poetry of molecular parsings whose alphabet is the periodic table' are all fractally implicated in one another.[116]

It is in such a 'materialist understanding of text' and in the 'understand[ing] of matter through the figure of the text in general' that Derrida's work offers the potential for a 'deconstructive materialism'[117] that would undo the very oppositions between the human and the non-human, nature and culture, the 'inside' and the 'outside,' that critics of deconstruction continue to rely on in their work. In a materialist understanding of Derridean thought, there is *no* '*outside*' not because we are all imprisoned in language and in systems of meaning that prohibit us from accessing what Meillassoux calls 'the great outdoors'; it is because this very outdoors is implicated and entangled in the beings that we ourselves are. For Kirby, Derrida's work opens up ways of thinking that are not predicated on an opposition or a division between the human and the non-human and that do not 'corral the subject from the object, or culture from nature, as if the difference is clear and the problem is answered in terms of dependence or independence; correlation or the lack of it.'[118] Kirby takes aim at the 'tendency to posit two separate entities or systems'—the human and its 'outside,' nature and culture—and instead finds within Derrida's notion of a general text 'a sense of "materiality"' that contests 'the actual identity of these terms and their respective contexts, circumscriptions and capacities.'[119] For Kirby, Derrida's assertion that there is 'no outside text' could be better glossed as 'there is no outside nature,' because nature is *itself* 'literate, numerate and social';[120] it is itself a manifestation or an expression of a general field of textuality in which 'differences are cut from the same cloth—they are all of a piece.'[121] This is not some anthropomorphic projection of human language and human textuality onto an outside world but a recognition of the way in which this so-called outside shares an intimate relationship with the supposed 'inside' of human discursive structures and systems of meaning.

What links human meaning to the wider manifestations of material difference within the so-called natural world is, for Martin Hägglund, contained within the Derridean notion of the trace. Responding to Meillassoux's critique of correlationism, Hägglund argues that 'the structure of the trace'— 'the co-implication of time and space' that Derrida recognises in the workings of language in the essay "Différance"—is 'the condition for everything that is temporal.'[122] Operating within and outside of human language and human systems of meaning, the structure of the trace is implicit in 'everything that is subjected to succession [. . .], whether it is alive or not'; it is implicit 'in the temporality of the living' as well as 'in the disintegration of inanimate matter.'[123] For Hägglund, the notion of the trace can thus 'serve to elucidate philosophical stakes in the understanding of the relation between the living and the nonliving that have been handed down to us by modern science,' allowing us to better understand the relations of continuity and difference that bind 'life and nonliving matter.'[124] Drawing on the example of decaying radioactive isotopes—an example that Meillassoux himself uses when referring to an ancestral past that would predate life and consciousness and remain exterior to the supposed correlationist paradigms of philosophical thought— Hägglund describes a 'continuity' between life and matter that differentially extends to human language and consciousness.[125] Such a reading of the trace outside of the traditional opposition between life and matter, the animate and the inanimate, the living and the non-living, opens up the possibility of what Richard Iveson describes as a 'radical and far-reaching critique' that would make of deconstruction a truly 'material and posthumanist praxis.'[126]

It is such a reconceptualisation of the relationship between language, life and matter that drives my own discussions of the anthropocenic trace. In my efforts to develop a non-anthropocentric reading of the notion of the lithic trace of the Anthropocene, I mobilise the Derridean concepts of *spectrality* and *survivance* to examine the differential structure of what Hägglund describes as the 'continuity' of biological and material existence.[127] Drawing on Hägglund's description of the decay of radioactive isotopes as an example of the 'survival' implicit in the structure of the trace,[128] I show how anthropogenic markings in the earth's strata can be read as expressions of a rich inter- and intra-relationality that 'lives' and 'lives on' in the entanglements of matter. In my reading, 'spectrality' and 'survivance' do not simply refer to 'the shifting margins of life and death'[129]—to the way that life is always inhabited by death and death by life, and to the way that mortal existence is lived as a haunting that moves 'from one moment to another,' always marked by what has passed and what is to come.[130] As developed in my readings of Derrida, these two terms point instead to a more fundamental haunting that emerges out of the material, biological and discursive entanglements by which *any* entity—human or non-human, linguistic or not, alive or inanimate—exists, subsists and persists. Iveson notes that in Derrida's work the notion of spectrality serves primarily to problematise the distinction between 'the living and the *no-longer* living,' whereas what is needed is an interrogation of the more fundamental opposition between the living and the '*not-yet* or *never* living.'[131] Spectrality is not merely, as Hägglund notes, 'an indispensable feature of life in general';[132] it points to the material processes by which *anything* and *everything* can survive, persist or endure—never alone and never singly, every material presence being actualised in and through otherness.

A Guide to What Follows

The anthropocentric logic that structures the notion of the Anthropocene manifests itself in two interrelated ways: firstly, through the positing of an anthropomorphic gaze that projects itself into the future in order to look back upon the present as past, and, secondly, through the assumption that certain geological markings in the strata of the earth will survive into the future as spectral traces of the human immortalised in the rock, continuing to bear witness to the significance of the human even in the face of its own absence. This book is structured around an analysis and a critique of these two gestures. The first part of the book (including this introduction and the chapter that follows it) outlines how and why the future-retrospectivity of the Anthropocene must be rethought, while the rest of the chapters attempt to enact this rethinking through an exploration of the material spectrality and survivance of the anthropocenic trace.

Chapter 1 begins with an examination of the way that the logic of future-retrospectivity manifests itself in several scientific and cultural discourses and practices of our time, and it shows how this logic can serve as a specular device that undermines the possibility for any true change. Examining arguments on both sides of what has come to be known as the 'good' and the 'bad' Anthropocene debate, the chapter demonstrates how many discourses on the Anthropocene adopt rhetorical strategies that project the anthropocentric structures of the present onto an imagined future in ways that continue to legitimise and affirm them. Despite their various proclamations of a rupture in human history and their calls for the creation of new worlds that would completely transform human-earth relations, many anthropocenic discourses presume a continuity between the present and the future that is predicated on the survival and continued presence of human beings upon this earth. Even when these discourses do not overtly envisage the continued survival of the human species—indeed, even when they consider the possibility of human extinction—the future-retrospective gestures they adopt continue to presume the existence of an anthropomorphic gaze that colonises the future and reflects the present back at itself unchallenged and unchanged.

The circularity of this logic has serious implications, not only for the way in which the future is *envisaged* but also for the way in which it is actively *shaped*. Having critiqued the anthropocentrism that underlies discourses on the Anthropocene, the first chapter goes on to examine how certain environmental projects are structured according to an archival logic that implicitly echoes the future-retrospectivity of the Anthropocene. The Frozen Ark initiative,[133] for instance, and the Svalbard Global Seed Vault[134] approach the present as a future trace or relic of itself—as a past that might be able to be recovered and reproduced in times to come. These projects are intended to protect the earth from further future biodiversity loss by preserving seeds, embryos and DNA samples from many non-human species in the hopes of being able to resurrect and revive them in the years, decades and centuries to come. But, as I show in my analysis, through the very practices they adopt, these projects do far more than merely preserve the frozen contents of their vaults. Alongside their preserved biological samples, they also reproduce and project into the future certain conceptions of what life is, how it functions and why it has value. These assumptions can be said to reflect the wider values of an anthropocentric and predominantly Western cultural imaginary that, within the context of these projects, works to shape the earth's biological future.

These preservation projects are governed by a future-retrospective logic that projects and reproduces the present—and with it a particular understanding of what constitutes *living presence*—into an unknown future. The biological preservation and conservation of tissue samples and specimens is largely predicated on an understanding of life as being autonomous and isolatable—as consisting of bodies that can be extracted from their environments, or of groups of organisms whose future presence can be contained and guaranteed in the archived samples of their genetic code. What is protected and preserved by these projects is the *presence* of certain lifeforms—their continued presence in time, certainly, but also their perceived presence as singular units of life that are easily distinguishable from their external environments. As I show in my analysis, however, the induced states of cryobiosis that such preservation projects rely on also tell a *different* story of presence and absence. Chapter 1 concludes with a consideration of how cryobiotic states draw attention to the *spectrality* of the living, revealing all forms of life to be always intimately implicated and entangled in that which they supposedly are not. This spectrality, I argue, underwrites all forms of living and non-living matter in ways that should compel us to rethink notions of presence and absence as they relate to the Anthropocene.

This attempt to rethink presence is taken up in Chapter 2 through a critique of one of the most predominant tropes of the anthropocenic imaginary—the idea that the current presence of human beings upon the earth is being inscribed in the strata like some anthropogenic signature or written mark. Zeroing in on the use of such textual metaphors in the scientific and cultural discourses surrounding the Anthropocene, I argue that rather than viewing the anthropocenic trace as a sign that has meaning for the human—as a mark of human presence or absence that is legible within a human semiotic framework—we should seek to develop a *materialist* understanding of the trace that is not predicated on the presumed presence or absence of human beings upon the earth, whether as producers, receivers or referents of the anthropocenic sign. This chapter lays the groundwork for such a reading through a problematisation of the notion of metaphor. It argues that any truly materialist reading of the Anthropocene must begin not merely with a reconceptualisation of the nature of *matter*, as is often seen in different permutations of new materialist thought, but with a rigorous re-evaluation of the nature of *language*. It is here that Derrida's notion of a 'general writing' or a general textuality proves useful. Through a reading of the recently published *Life Death* seminar, first delivered by Derrida in 1975–1976, this chapter shows how metaphors of textual inscription function as 'more than' simple representationalist tropes because they are themselves implicated in the different material realities they are supposed to represent. Drawing on the work of Karen Barad, I argue that Derrida's notion of textuality functions as a 'diffractive' paradigm that reveals inherent relationships of difference (and *différance*) between language and reality, meaning and matter, that cannot be reduced to a human representationalist framework.

This 'diffractive' reading of textuality (and of textuality *as* a diffractive paradigm) provides us with a language with which to think the anthropocenic trace not as a representational sign *of* the human that can be read *by* the human but as a primarily *lithic* inscription that is formed out of complex interactions between different forms of matter. As a diffractive paradigm, the notion of textuality reveals the ways in which different material realities are always implied and implicated in one another, and it allows us to question the binary oppositions and divisions to which these rich relationships of difference have traditionally been reduced. My analysis shows how this textuality is not merely something that can be said to be *present*, whether in language, in living organisms or in material entities, precisely because it marks the way in which all of these entities are always constituted out of relationships of difference and otherness; it marks the ways in which they are always implicated in that which they supposedly are not. These movements of textuality constitute intra-active relationships *between*, *within* and *amongst* entities that allow for the existence of different material realities. And, as it is used here, the *notion* of textuality *itself* also cuts across any simple opposition between the human and the non-human, the living and the non-living, the animate and the inanimate, itself thus also engaging in such intra-active movements of difference and deferral.

It is from within this understanding of textuality that the rest of the book approaches the notion of an anthropocenic inscription. Chapter 3 shows how the paradigm of textuality, as it is developed through my analysis, opens up the space for a rethinking of other related concepts, including notions of *life* and *survival*. Drawing on Derrida's conceptualisation of a spectral 'living on' that can push beyond the boundaries of life and death, presence and absence, while also cutting across the distinction between the animate and the inanimate, I explore the possibility of a *material survivance* that 'lives' or at least 'lives on' in the processes by which non-living matter interacts with other living and non-living entities within its environment. This survivance is not some kind of quality or characteristic of either the living or the non-living—it cannot be thought of as something that *belongs* to an entity or that constitutes its *essence*. What the notion of survivance draws attention to is the way that every entity, every phenomenon and indeed every concept (including that of *survivance* itself) is always constituted out of intra-active relationships with its environment, and it shows that it is precisely in these entanglements that such entities can exist and persist.

The paradigms of textuality and survivance allow us to see how something like a radioactive isotope can 'live' and 'live on' through its *inscriptions* in the bodies and material environments it comes into contact with. This is significant for my reading of the Anthropocene because radioactive isotopes embedded in rock and soil sediments from the fallout from the use of nuclear weapons in the second half of the 20th century are widely considered to be the most likely candidates for an anthropocenic trace that will survive in the strata of the earth in the distant future. Radioactive materials are not biological organisms and neither are they linguistic entities, but they can be shown to enact forms of material survivance that are *conceptually comparable to* as well as *materially entangled in* the survivance of biological and discursive processes. Chapter 4 explores how such a diffractive understanding of material survivance invites us to rethink the notion of anthropocenic inscription. It does so through a materialist close reading that tracks how radioactive isotopes survive through their own decay, through chemical mutations and transformations that also transform the environments they come in to contact with. These intra-active transformations transgress the boundaries between different material states, different bodies and different species, across various biological, ecological and social realities, creating complex cascading entanglements that echo across time and space. I argue that tracking these entangled movements of survivance is crucial because it can allow us to reassess the value and significance that we attribute to different biological and material realities, and it can allow us to better understand our own entanglements in them. Such thought can provide us with the tools to reconceptualise our understanding of the Anthropocene, but beyond that, it can also provide us with a better *language* with which to engage and participate in the diverse and complex realities that constitute the present by showing us that the way we *think* and *speak* about these realities is always transformatively entangled within them.

Notes

1. Günther Anders, "Language and End Time (Sections I, IV and V of 'Sprache und Endzeit')," trans. Christopher John Müller, *Thesis Eleven* 153, no. 1 (August 2019): 135, https://doi.org/10.1177/0725513619864448.

2. Günther Anders, "Reflections on the H Bomb," *Dissent* 3, no. 2 (Spring 1956): 149.

3. See, for instance, Déborah Danowski and Eduardo Viveiros de Castro, *The Ends of the World*, trans. Rodrigo Guimaraes Nunes (Cambridge: Polity, 2016), 4; Jean-Pierre Dupuy, *A Short Treatise on the Metaphysics of Tsunamis*, trans. M. B. DeBevoise (East Lansing: Michigan State University Press, 2015); and Christopher John Müller, "From Radioactivity to Data Mining: Günther Anders in the Anthropocene," *Thesis Eleven* 153, no. 1 (August 2019), https://doi.org/10.1177/0725513619867180.

4. Srećko Horvat, *After the Apocalypse* (Cambridge: Polity, 2021), 9–10.

5. As Karen Barad reminds us in her reflections on the destruction of the Marshall Islands in the nuclear tests conducted by the United States between 1946 and 1958, for many people around the world the nuclear apocalypse has already occurred (Karen Barad, "After the End of the World: Entangled Nuclear Colonialisms, Matters of Force, and the Material Force of Justice," *Theory & Event* 22, no. 3 (July 2019): 537–38). The same is true of climate change. Rising sea levels have already washed away villages on islands in the South Pacific, millions of people have died and been displaced as a result of climate-related disasters in Bangladesh, and the crises in Yemen and Syria are believed to have been brought on, in part, by drought (Denise Chow, "Three Islands Disappeared in the Past Year. Is Climate Change to Blame?" *NBC News*, June 9, 2019, https://www.nbcnews.com/mach/science/three-islands-disappeared-past-year-climate-change-blame-ncna1015316; "Climate Displacement in Bangladesh," Environmental Justice Foundation, accessed June 15, 2021, https://ejfoundation.org/reports/climate-displacement-in-bangladesh; Collin Douglas, "A Storm Without Rain: Yemen, Water, Climate Change, and Conflict," The Center for Climate and Security, August 3, 2016, https://climateandsecurity.org/2016/08/a-storm-without-rain-yemen-water-climate-change-and-conflict/).

6. For more on this see Bruno Latour, "Agency at the Time of the Anthropocene," *New Literary History* 45, no. 1 (2014): 1–18, https://doi.org/10.1353/nlh.2014.0003; Ulrich Beck, *World at Risk*, trans. Ciaran Cronin (Cambridge: Polity, 2009); and Timothy Morton, *Hyperobjects: Philosophy and Ecology After the End of the World* (Minneapolis: University of Minnesota Press, 2013).

7. Joanna Zylinska, *The End of Man: A Feminist Counterapocalypse* (Minneapolis: University of Minnesota Press, 2018), 64.

8. Anders, "Reflections," 149.

9. Horvat, *After the Apocalypse*, 32.

10. Dipesh Chakrabarty, "The Climate of History: Four Theses," *Critical Inquiry* 35, no. 2 (Winter 2009): 197, https://doi.org/10.1086/596640.

11. David Wood, *Deep Time, Dark Times: On Being Geologically Human* (New York: Fordham University Press, 2019), 18.

12. Wood, *Deep Time, Dark Times*, 66, 71.

13. Jacques Derrida, *Specters of Marx: The State of the Debt, the Work of Mourning, and the New International*, trans. Peggy Kamuf (New York: Routledge, 1994), 3.

14. Günther Anders, "Theses for the Atomic Age," *The Massachusetts Review* 3, no. 3 (Spring 1962): 493.

15. Dupuy, *Short Treatise*, 46.

16. Dupuy, *Short Treatise*, 9.

17. Horvat, *After the Apocalypse*, 4.

18. As widely documented in the media, one of the most common side-effects of months of lockdown was that of 'losing track of time': of time itself becoming displaced and unaccounted for (see, for instance, Kelsey Borresen, "The Psychology Behind Why We Lose Track of Time in Quarantine," *HuffPost*, April 24, 2020, https://www.huffpost.com/entry/psychology-time-quarantine_l_5e9e2095c5b6b2e5b 836de6d; Olivia Petter, "Is It Monday or Wednesday? Why Lockdown Confuses Our Sense of Time," *Independent*, May 4, 2020, https://www.independent.co.uk/life-style/ lockdown-time-day-week-forget-why-confused-psychology-coronavirus-a9497901 .html). But the sense of temporal displacement that defines pandemic life extends beyond this. The logic of risk assessment that was drilled into our daily lives dictated that one always behave as if one were already exposed, counting days backwards and forwards in two-week quarantine blocks, aware that the reality of today would only be disclosed in the days and weeks to come. This spectral sense of the present, perceived retrospectively from the future, is at the heart of what I will be referring to in what follows as the future-retro-vision of the anthropocenic imaginary.

19. Horvat, *After the Apocalypse*, 8–9, 40–41.

20. Karen Barad, "Troubling Time/s and Ecologies of Nothingness: Re-turning, Re-membering, and Facing the Incalculable," *New Formations: A Journal of Culture/ Theory/Politics* 92 (2018): 57, https://doi.org/10.3898/NEWF:92.05.2017.

21. Barad, "Troubling Time/s," 58.

22. Barad, "Troubling Time/s," 58. Discussing the 2018 IPCC Special Report on Global Warming, Jemma Deer notes that 'what is perhaps most disturbing [. . .] is not the promised monstrosity of a world "no longer recognisable," but rather the realisation that much of what is being described here (heatwaves, droughts, increased extinction rates, fires) has already begun to occur' (Jemma Deer, "Quenched: Five Fires for Thinking Extinction," *The Oxford Literary Review* 41, no. 1 (July 2019): 3, https://doi.org/10.3366/olr.2019.0262). As Frédéric Neyrat puts it, when we look back at ourselves through the speculative lens of the future, all that we can truly see is thus the 'haunting' image of our own extinction (Frédéric Neyrat, "Ghosts of Extinction: An Essay in Spectral Ecopolitics," *The Oxford Literary Review* 41, no. 1 (July 2019): 58, https://doi.org/10.3366/olr.2019.0267).

23. Anders, "Theses," 493.

24. Joseph Masco, *The Nuclear Borderlands: The Manhattan Project in Post–Cold War New Mexico* (Princeton, NJ: Princeton University Press, 2006), 27–28.

25. Masco, *Nuclear Borderlands*, 12.

26. Horvat, *After the Apocalypse*, 11–12. Horvat borrows the phrase 'naked apocalypse' from Anders, who argues that the nuclear threat is the threat of absolute 'nothingness,' of a complete annihilation of both past and future (Anders, "Reflections," 148–49). I will be drawing on the idea of 'nothingness' in what follows in order to explore the implications of the spectrality I am outlining here and consider how it can and should be thought differently.

27. Horvat, *After the Apocalypse*, 9, 50.

28. Mark O'Connell, *Notes from an Apocalypse: A Personal Journey to the End of the World and Back* (London: Granta, 2020), 238.

29. O'Connell, *Notes*, 4. Horvat similarly describes the present as a 'flashback coming not from the past, but from the future,' in which despite still being 'here in the "present,"' one is 'already transposed into the future' from where 'the unfolding present' appears 'as something that is already past' (Horvat, *After the Apocalypse*, 49–50).

30. O'Connell, *Notes*, 194, 184.

31. O'Connell, *Notes*, 206.

32. O'Connell, *Notes*, 195–96.

33. From this perspective, the writer imagines his belongings 'undergoing [their] own afterlife of decay and dissolution' (*Notes*, 196), and when he returns home from his trip, transformed by his experiences like some modern-day Gulliver, he turns his telescoped gaze onto the world around him, viewing his house and his neighbourhood in Dublin as composed of similar aging fragments of the past.

34. Claire Colebrook, *Death of the PostHuman: Essays on Extinction*, Vol. 1. (Ann Arbor, MI: Open Humanities Press, 2015), 24.

35. For more on this see, for instance, Gregg Mitman, "Hubris or Humility? Genealogies of the Anthropocene," in *Future Remains: A Cabinet of Curiosities for the Anthropocene*, ed. Gregg Mitman, Marco Armiero, and Robert S. Emmett (Chicago: University of Chicago Press, 2018); and Dale Jamieson, "The Anthropocene; Love It or Leave It," in *The Routledge Companion to the Environmental Humanities*, ed. Ursula K. Heise, Jon Christensen, and Michelle Niemann (London: Routledge, 2017).

36. Clive Hamilton, *Defiant Earth: The Fate of Humans in the Anthropocene* (London: Polity, 2017), 41. Hamilton argues that anthropocentrism constitutes 'a scientific fact' rather than 'a normative claim': human beings *are* 'the dominant creature, so dominant that [they] have shifted the geological arc of the planet' (Hamilton, *Defiant Earth*, 43). In a certain sense this is true: as David Farrier notes, in the Anthropocene human beings have recreated the earth in their image, turning it into an anthropomorphic 'mirror' to see themselves in (David Farrier, *Footprints: In Search of Future Fossils* (New York: Farrar, Straus and Giroux, 2020), 47). But this is not quite the whole picture. As Mitman reminds us, it is myopic and hubristic 'to suggest

that we are the only species that has reshaped life on earth' (Mitman, "Hubris or Humility," 61), and if there is one thing that the environmental crises we face have indeed revealed, it is precisely that we are less masters of the earth than subjects to it (Jamieson, "The Anthropocene; Love It or Leave It," 15).

37. For more on this see Zylinska, *The End of Man*, 9–12; and Tom Cohen, Claire Colebrook, and J. Hillis Miller, *Twilight of the Anthropocene Idols* (London: Open Humanities Press, 2016), 86.

38. Derrida, *Specters of Marx*, 25.

39. Jacques Derrida, "Différance," in *Margins of Philosophy*, trans. Alan Bass (Brighton, UK: Harvester Press, 1982), 13.

40. Jacques Derrida, *The Beast and the Sovereign*, Vol. 2, trans. Geoffrey Bennington (Chicago: University of Chicago Press, 2011), 50–51.

41. Michael Naas, *The End of the World and Other Teachable Moments: Jacques Derrida's Final Seminar* (New York: Fordham University Press, 2015), 64.

42. Derrida, "Différance," 13.

43. Barad, "After the End of the World," 539; emphasis added.

44. See the 'exordium' to *Specters of Marx*, as well as Derrida's final interview, *Learning to Live Finally*, trans. Pascale-Anne Brault and Michael Naas (Hoboken, NJ: Melville House, 2007).

45. The phrase is taken from Roy Scranton's *Learning to Die in the Anthropocene: Reflections on the End of a Civilization* (San Francisco: City Lights Books, 2015). As I show in my readings of Derrida in the chapters that follow, life and death are intimately entangled with one another, and any appeal to 'life' ought to be understood as encompassing this entanglement.

46. Vincent Ialenti, *Deep Time Reckoning: How Future Thinking Can Help Earth Now* (Cambridge, MA: MIT Press, 2020), xvi–1.

47. E. Ann Kaplan, *Climate Trauma: Foreseeing the Future in Dystopian Film and Fiction* (New Brunswick, NJ: Rutgers University Press, 2016), 1.

48. Rob Nixon, "All Tomorrow's Warnings," *Public Books*, August 13, 2020, https://www.publicbooks.org/all-tomorrows-warnings/.

49. Nixon, "Tomorrow."

50. Greta Thunberg, UN Climate Change COP24 Conference (Katowice, 2018), https://www.youtube.com/watch?v=VFkQSGyeCWg&ab_channel=Connect4 Climate.

51. Naomi Oreskes and Erik Conway, *The Collapse of Western Civilization: A View from the Future* (New York: Columbia University Press, 2014), xi.

52. Kaplan, *Climate Trauma*, xix.

53. Jean-Pierre Dupuy, "The Precautionary Principle and Enlightened Doomsaying: Rational Choice Before the Apocalypse," *Occasion: Interdisciplinary Studies in the Humanities* 1, no. 1 (October 2009).

54. Dupuy, "Enlightened Doomsaying," 8.

55. Dupuy, "Enlightened Doomsaying," 10.

56. Anders, "Thesis," 498–99; Anders, "Reflections," 158.

57. Dupuy, "Enlightened Doomsaying," 10.

58. Dupuy, *Short Treatise*, 7.

59. Nixon, "Tomorrow."

60. Dupuy, *Short Treatise*, 3.

61. Günther Anders, "Die beweinte Zukunft," in *Die atomare Drohung: Radikale Überlegungen zum atomaren Zeitalter* (Munich: C. H. Beck, 2003), 1–10. All quoted passages are translated from the German by Christopher John Müller.

62. Emphasis added.

63. Nixon, "Tomorrow."

64. Emphasis added.

65. Perhaps the most evocative description of this can be found in Anders's "Commandments in the Atomic Age," which begins as follows:

> Your first thought upon awakening be: 'Atom.' For you should not begin your day with the illusion that what surrounds you is a stable world. Already to-morrow it can be 'something that only has been': for we, you, and I and our fellow men are 'more mortal' and 'more temporal' than all who, until yesterday, had been considered mortal. 'More mortal' because our temporality means not only that we are mortal, not only that we are 'killable.' That 'custom' has always existed. But that we, as *mankind*, are 'killable.' And 'mankind' doesn't mean only to-day's mankind, not only mankind spread over the provinces of our globe; but also mankind spread over the provinces of time. For if the mankind of to-day is killed, then that which *has* been, dies with it; and the mankind to come too. The mankind which *has been* because, where there is no one who remembers, there will be nothing left to remember; and the mankind to come, because where there is no to-day, no to-morrow can become a to-day. The door in front of us bears the inscription: 'Nothing will have been'; and from within: 'Time was an episode.' Not, however, as our ancestors had hoped, an episode between two eternities; but one between two nothingnesses; between the nothingness of that which, remembered by no one, will have been as though it had never been, and the nothingness of that which will never be. And as there will be no one to tell one nothingness from the other, they will melt into one single nothingness. This, then, is the completely new, the apocalyptic kind of temporality, our temporality, compared with which everything we had called 'temporal' has become a bagatelle. Therefore your first thought after awakening be: 'Atom.'

(Günther Anders, "Commandments in the Atomic Age," in *Philosophy and Technology: Readings in the Philosophical Problems of Technology*, ed. Carl Mitcham and Robert Mackey (New York: Free Press, 1972), 130).

66. Anders, "Reflections," 149.

67. Chakrabarty, "Climate of History," 221, 198.

68. Alan Weisman, *The World Without Us* (London: Virgin Books, 2007), 4.

69. Chakrabarty, "Climate of History," 197.

70. Chakrabarty, "Climate of History," 197–98.

71. Noah Heringman, "The Anthropocene Reads Buffon; or, Reading Like Geology," in *Anthropocene Reading: Literary History in Geologic Times*, ed. Tobias Menely

and Jesse Oak Taylor (University Park: Pennsylvania State University Press, 2017), 60–61.

72. Weisman, *World Without Us*, 65, 124, 133, 154.

73. Weisman, *World Without Us*, 111.

74. Michael Madsen, *Into Eternity: A Film for the Future* (Lise Lense-Møller, 2010).

75. This would constitute an example of what Eugene Thacker describes as a moment 'in which thinking enigmatically confronts the horizon of its own possibility—the thought of the unthinkable' (Eugene Thacker, *In the Dust of This Planet* (Winchester, UK: Zero Books, 2011), 2).

76. Wood, *Deep Time, Dark Times*, 15.

77. Cohen, Colebrook, and Miller, *Twilight*, 9.

78. Cohen, Colebrook, and Miller, *Twilight*, 23.

79. Cohen, Colebrook, and Miller, *Twilight*, 23.

80. Cohen, Colebrook, and Miller, *Twilight*, 59.

81. Cohen, Colebrook, and Miller, *Twilight*, 82, 114–15.

82. Cohen, Colebrook, and Miller, *Twilight*, 23, 59.

83. As I show in more detail in Chapter 1, geologists and writers on the Anthropocene frequently resort to this anthropomorphic trope, with Diane Ackerman, for instance, conjuring up 'a future geologist' named Olivine through which to filter her tale of human beings leaving their 'signature everywhere' on the earth (Diane Ackerman, *The Human Age: The World Shaped by Us* (New York: Norton, 2014), 34–35). The geologist Jan Zalasiewicz similarly imagines a 'post-human future' in which 'extra-terrestrial explorers or colonists,' or even 'a new, home-grown intelligence,' find and decipher the 'final footprint' of human beings on the planet (Jan Zalasiewicz, *The Earth After Us: What Legacy Will Humans Leave in the Rocks?* (Oxford: Oxford University Press, 2008), 1, 3).

84. For more on the use of this term, see the contributions to Jason W. Moore, ed., *Anthropocene or Capitalocene? Nature, History, and the Crisis of Capitalism* (Oakland, CA: PM Press, 2016).

85. Eileen Crist and Helen Kopnina, "Unsettling Anthropocentrism," *Dialectical Anthropology* 38 (December 2014): 388, https://doi.org/10.1007/s10624-014-9362-1.

86. Kathryn Yusoff, *A Billion Black Anthropocenes or None* (Minneapolis: University of Minnesota Press, 2018), xii.

87. Crist and Kopnina, "Unsettling Anthropocentrism," 388.

88. Anders, "Reflections," 149.

89. Madsen, *Into Eternity*.

90. Anders, "Theses," 496; emphasis added.

91. Anders, "Reflections," 149.

92. Stacy Alaimo and Susan Heckman, eds., *Material Feminisms* (Bloomington: Indiana University Press, 2008), 9.

93. Diana Coole and Samantha Frost, eds., *New Materialisms: Ontology, Agency, and Politics* (Durham, NC: Duke University Press, 2010), 6.

94. Donna J. Haraway, *Staying with the Trouble: Making Kin in the Chthulucene* (Durham, NC: Duke University Press, 2016), 1.

95. Karen Barad, *Meeting the Universe Halfway: Quantum Physics and the Entanglement of Matter and Meaning* (Durham, NC: Duke University Press, 2007), 214.

96. Barad, *Meeting the Universe*, 218–19.

97. See, for instance, Simon L. Lewis and Mark A. Maslin, "Defining the Anthropocene," *Nature* 519, no. 7542 (March 2015): 171, https://doi.org/10.1038/nature14258.

98. Coole and Frost, *New Materialisms*, 3.

99. Coole and Frost, *New Materialisms*, 3.

100. Coole and Frost, *New Materialisms*, 3.

101. Alaimo and Heckman, *Material Feminisms*, 2.

102. Alaimo and Heckman, *Material Feminisms*, 3–4.

103. Martin Hägglund, "Radical Atheist Materialism: A Critique of Meillassoux," in Levi Bryant, Nick Srnicek, and Graham Harman, eds., *The Speculative Turn: Continental Materialism and Realism* (Melbourne: re.press, 2011), 115.

104. Quentin Meillassoux, *After Finitude: An Essay on the Necessity of Contingency*, trans. Ray Brassier (London: Continuum, 2008), 5, 7.

105. Meillassoux, *After Finitude*, 7.

106. Meillassoux, *After Finitude*, 7.

107. Meillassoux, *After Finitude*, 27.

108. Meillassoux, *After Finitude*, 9, 50.

109. Meillassoux, *After Finitude*, 51, 38.

110. Jonathan Basile, "Misreading Generalised Writing: From Foucault to Speculative Realism and New Materialism," *Oxford Literary Review* 40, no. 1 (July 2018): 26, https://doi.org/10.3366/olr.2018.0236.

111. Jacques Derrida, *Of Grammatology*, trans. Gayatri Chakravorty Spivak (corrected ed.) (Baltimore: Johns Hopkins University Press, 1998), 158.

112. See Basile "Misreading" for a further overview of how this phrase has been, and continues to be misread.

113. Matthias Fritsch, Philippe Lynes, and David Wood, eds., *Eco-Deconstruction: Derrida and Environmental Philosophy* (New York: Fordham University Press, 2018), 7.

114. Fritsch, Lynes, and Wood, *Eco-Deconstruction*, 8.

115. Pheng Cheah, "Non-Dialectical Materialism," in Coole and Frost, *New Materialisms*, 73.

116. Vicki Kirby, *Quantum Anthropologies: Life at Large* (Durham, NC: Duke University Press, 2011), 13, 41.

117. Cheah, "Non-Dialectical Materialism," 73–74.

118. Vicki Kirby, "Matter Out of Place: 'New Materialism' in Review," in *What if Culture Was Nature All Along*, ed. Vicki Kirby (Edinburgh: Edinburgh University Press, 2017), 14.

119. Kirby, "Matter Out of Place," 14.

120. Vicki Kirby, "Foreword," in *What if Culture*, ix.

121. Kirby, "Matter Out of Place," 8.

122. Hägglund, "Radical Atheist Materialism," 118–19.

123. Hägglund, "Radical Atheist Materialism," 119.

124. Hägglund, "Radical Atheist Materialism," 119.

125. Hägglund, "Radical Atheist Materialism," 123–24.

126. Richard Iveson, "Being Without Life: On the Trace of Organic Chauvinism with Derrida and DeLanda," in *Philosophy After Nature*, ed. Rosi Braidotti and Rick Dolphijn (London: Rowman & Littlefield International, 2017), 180–81. Although Iveson detects in Hägglund's work traces of the same 'organic chauvinism' and 'late-stage vitalism' that he identifies in Derrida's own writings—a 'dominant zoo-centrism that bestows exceptional ontological status upon the living'—he nevertheless draws on Hägglund's reading to show how Derrida's work offers the potential for a thorough reconceptualisation of material existence that would push deconstruction beyond its 'zoocentric privilege' (Iveson, "Being Without Life," 179, 189).

127. Hägglund, "Radical Atheist Materialism," 119, 123.

128. Hägglund, "Radical Atheist Materialism," 123.

129. Michael Marder, *Plant Thinking: A Philosophy of Vegetal Life* (New York: Columbia University Press, 2013), 52.

130. Hägglund, "Radical Atheist Materialism," 127.

131. Iveson, "Being Without Life," 188.

132. Hägglund, "Radical Atheist Materialism," 127.

133. Frozen Ark, https://www.frozenark.org/.

134. Svalbard Global Seed Vault, https://www.seedvault.no/.

CHAPTER ONE

~

Preservation and Stasis

The Anthropocene Echo-Chamber

In our contemporary cultural imaginary, the concept of the Anthropocene functions primarily as a mirror: it is a specular device that reproduces the image of the 'human,' allowing us to contemplate our continued presence and survival upon this earth. Despite the fact that the Anthropocene appears to open up the possibility of engaging with a remote and necessarily unknowable future, this concept remains, as Sverker Sörlin notes, all 'about the now.'[1] Joanna Zylinska describes the Anthropocene as an 'epistemological filter through which we humans can see ourselves,' one that has 'triggered the production of multiple images and narratives about ourselves and the world around us.'[2] In this sense, as Mary Louise Pratt argues, the Anthropocene can be thought of as a Bakhtinian *chronotope*, as 'a particular configuration of time and space that generates stories through which society can examine itself.'[3] The notion of the Anthropocene does not merely refer to a geological epoch in the earth's history; this term and the future-retro-vision it invites function as scientific and cultural paradigms that the present-day Western world can identify and define itself in. As Tobias Menely and Jesse Oak Taylor note, the Anthropocene is 'an epoch in Earth's geohistory defined by the shaping influence of human activity,' but it is also the cultural condition by which 'our singular species' becomes increasingly aware of its impact upon the earth and is driven to read '*itself* in the rocks' so as to establish 'new stories about its identity and this planet.'[4]

These stories are dominated, in one form or another, by a belief in our continued survival: the survival of our species, or, at least, of our legacy.

Several critics and theorists have noted that while the extreme timescales opened up by the thought of the Anthropocene appear to confront human beings with the very real possibility of their own collective demise, the discourses that shape this geological and cultural paradigm remain unmistakably structured by a rhetoric of redemption that grants human beings final victory over death and extinction through the preservation and persistence of their memory. For Zylinska, the Anthropocene functions as a masculinist, Christian paradigm that holds the promise of immortal redemption,[5] while Claire Colebrook claims that in the specular self-diagnosis of the Anthropocene, 'the human becomes at once victim, agent and redeemer.'[6] In Bronislaw Szerszynski's assessment, the 'truth of the Anthropocene is less about what humanity is doing, than the traces that humanity will leave behind.'[7] These traces function as a *'memento mori,'* reminding us of the inevitability of our own deaths while also providing proof of our continued survival. As Szerszynski explains it, 'the fate of "man" in the Anthropocene is not that he will be erased, but that he will be made immortal, as a trace preserved forever in the rock.' The 'becoming geological of the human' does not merely mark the 'negation' of the human species; it also constitutes its final 'apotheosis.'[8] Seen through the future-retro-vision of the Anthropocene, human beings are immortalised in the traces they leave behind upon this earth—traces that bear witness to the continued presence of the human, even in the face of its supposed absence.

The promise of survival, redemption and immortality manifests itself most explicitly in the figure of the 'far-distant future reader,' which constitutes an 'indispensable' trope of the Anthropocene paradigm.[9] Jan Zalasiewicz's imagining of extra-terrestrial explorers, or even 'a newly evolved species of hyper-intelligent rodent,' discovering evidence of the current age buried in the Earth's rock,[10] draws attention to the way that the concept of the Anthropocene necessarily positions itself in the space of a future from which the human (or at least some form of anthropomorphic gaze) is able to survive and bear witness to the past.[11] Together with the notion of a human 'signature' in the earth's strata, this gaze is central to the entire anthropocenic imaginary. The notion of the Anthropocene is predicated on the assumption that there will, in the future, be someone or something left to recognise and name the current geological epoch. Even when the figure of a future geologist-explorer is not explicitly invoked, the paradigm of the Anthropocene remains conceptually structured by this trope and the future-retro-vision it invokes. In speculating on how the present may be viewed retrospectively in the future, the concept of the Anthropocene anticipates the existence of a *post*-Anthropocene world of geologists and stratigraphers who would be both willing and able to decipher the lithic messages of the past—a post-Anthropocene world, that is, that would be similar enough to our own for this geological concept to still have currency.

The Anthropocene is overwhelmingly about *us*: it is about the survival of the present—the *human* world of the present—into a speculative future. The cultural and scientific discourses and practices that shape this contemporary paradigm are structured by a circular and specular logic that reproduces and replicates the present, projecting it into the very same future that it attempts to look back at itself from. Dipesh Chakrabarty argues that the Anthropocene constitutes a break with the past—one that is 'deeply destructive of our general sense of history.'[12] But the Anthropocene is predicated on the possibility of *preservation*—on the preservation of our history in the strata of the earth and on the preservation of the scientific and cultural discourses and practices by which this history can be understood. The notion of the Anthropocene is based on the assumption that traces of human civilisation are being preserved in the strata of the earth for future geologists and stratigraphers to puzzle over and decipher. And for this act of preservation to have any significance—indeed, for it to *have taken place*—then the future must be structured in a way that will allow for these traces to be read. As I show in what follows, commentators on the Anthropocene might indeed claim that this geological concept draws attention to the possibility of the ultimate destruction of the human world as we know it and the possible creation of a radically different one. But in its conceptuality this notion remains tied to the expectation of a certain fundamental *stasis*—a continuity between the present and the future that allows for the one to be reflected in the other, foreclosing the possibility of any true change. Through the very future-retrospectivity of its logic, the notion of the Anthropocene projects aspects of the present onto the future, and it then uses this same projected future to reflect back on the present in a circular logic that always returns to the self-same.

Preservation always implies some form of stasis. Any act of archivisation works by suspending the present, freezing it in place, transforming it into that which *will have been*, in order for it to survive into the future, untouched and unscathed. And along with that which is archived, the very *structure* of the archive—what Derrida refers to as the 'place' and the 'law,' the 'substrate' and the 'authority' of the archive, the discourses and practices that give it shape[13]—must also be preserved. The archive does not merely protect its *contents*; through the act of preservation it also reproduces and projects *itself* into the future, ensuring enough continuity for its archival matter to be one day retrieved and revived. Viewed through the future-retrospectivity of the Anthropocene, the current moment appears as a fixed and already-archived past—as a spectral relic or remnant that is suspended in time and projected into the future with the hopes of being one day recuperated and redeemed. But this conceptual act of anthropocenic projection also hinges on the assumption that the same discourses and practices that structure the present will be in place in the future to welcome this geologically archived past. As I show in what follows, the discourses and practices of the Anthropocene seek, both intentionally and unintentionally, to structure and shape the future in a way that ensures continuity with the present world. The archival gesture of the Anthropocene and the specular logic that it sets into motion demand and enact the static preservation, projection and reproduction of the present into that which supposedly remains unknown and unknowable.

This chapter examines the implications of this circular and specular logic, exploring its workings in a variety of anthropocenic discourses and practices that seek to reflect on the present and forge new paths for the future. Exploring arguments on both sides of what has come to be known as the 'good' and the 'bad' Anthropocene debate, I show how both of these positions are implicitly structured by a future-retro-vision that projects the anthropocentric gaze of the present onto the future, foreclosing any possibility of radical change. Despite their various calls for a new world and a new humanity, many anthropocenic discourses continue to project the same capitalist logic, the same social structures, the same techno-scientific practices and the same anthropocentric values and assumptions that underlie the current world into the future, effectively transforming this future into a reflection of the present. Whether this is done to celebrate, validate and protect the present, or, conversely, to denounce, delegitimise and dismantle it is to a large extent irrelevant—the result remains the same: the future is hijacked and made to function as a foil or a mirror of the current world. The following sections explore the implications of this specular logic for our understanding of the Anthropocene and outline the need to develop alternative ways of thinking and living that can challenge the presumed centrality of the human upon this earth and its anthropocentric plans for the future.

Imagining the Future

This circular logic is in evidence in visions of the future put forward by a range of thinkers, writers and critics who attempt to make sense of the anthropocenic state of the present. Attitudes towards the Anthropocene vary from an acceptance and even a celebration of humankind's newfound status as a 'significant geological [and] morphological force' upon this planet, to quote one of the earliest descriptions of the Anthropocene,[14] to unequivocal denouncements and condemnations of the way that human beings have plundered and pillaged the earth. On one side of this debate, the Anthropocene is presented as an 'amazing opportunity' for human beings[15]—a feat of human exceptionalism and the natural culmination of a project of civilisation that began with the evolution of the human species—while on the other, the Anthropocene is denounced as the result of an unbridled hubris that will lead to the collective downfall of the human species. The two sides of this debate appear deeply and irrevocably entrenched in their differences: they hold diametrically opposed views on what should be deemed to be of value in human society, and they present radically different visions and ambitions for the future. But the two positions also share a surprisingly common rhetoric and employ strikingly similar gestures that undermine their various calls for radical change. On both sides of this debate, the current moment is viewed as constituting a significant threshold in the history of human civilisation, and the future is presented as holding the potential for a new world and even a new kind of humanity that will liberate us from the woes of the present. At the same time, this rhetoric of newness is undercut by a specular and circular logic in which the future functions as a mirror of the present. True to the spirit of the Anthropocene, these discourses may promise radical change and transformation, but what they actually deliver through the circular logic they employ is a specular engagement with the present that replicates and reproduces its basic structures.

In very different ways, both sides of this debate call for a transformation of the present into something new—a world fundamentally altered by geoengineering or one that radically divests itself of the burdens of human civilisation. For Erle Ellis and other self-proclaimed 'ecopragmatists and ecomodernists,'[16] the current moment constitutes 'the beginning of a new geological epoch ripe with human-directed opportunity,'[17] one defined by the possibility of 'a radical decoupling of humans from nature'[18] and a liberation from the material and ecological realities that have bound human beings to the earth.[19] These beliefs are anathema to thinkers on the other side of the Anthropocene debate, for whom it is the very myth of progress, the notion of human perfectibility and the belief that humankind is separate from nature that have led to the violent destruction of the earth and the crises faced today. But in their critiques, these thinkers also use a very similar rhetoric, identifying the present as a threshold moment in the history of civilisation and expressing hope for a new and transformed future. For proponents of the Dark Mountain Project, for instance, the current moment offers the potential for a 'massive change' that would result in 'the end of the world as we know it' and the creation of an 'uncivilised' future in which a new relationship to nature can be forged.[20] Meanwhile, for a thinker like Clive Hamilton, who positions himself somewhere between the two sides of this debate, denouncing the 'naïve hopefulness' of ecomodernists[21] while also rejecting the 'meekness' of their critics,[22] the Anthropocene also constitutes 'a new-world-in-the-making,' one that demands 'a new kind of human' able to acknowledge both the 'greatness of the human project' and the 'extreme danger that goes with it.'[23]

Despite the radical differences between these various positions, they are all predicated on the belief that the Anthropocene constitutes a break or a turning point of sorts, that it heralds the coming of a new age and a new world marked by a radically different relationship to the earth. But the rhetoric of 'newness' and radical change that is common to these discourses is undercut in all three instances by a shared anthropocenic logic that reproduces the present through the lens of the future and uses this imaginary future to legitimise and validate the present. This is in evidence in Erle Ellis's suggestion that 'in the distant future [. . .] we [might] be able to look back' at the world we have created 'with pride.'[24] Although Ellis claims that human beings should not 'look back' but should 'look ahead' in anticipation of the achievements of the future, in effect his writings *look forward* only in order to *look back*: they engage in a future-retrospective gaze that validates and legitimises the present by rerouting it through the specular lens of a supposedly new world. By referring to future human beings as 'we'—by wondering how 'we' might come to see ourselves in this distant future—Ellis further exemplifies how the future functions in his discourse as a simple projection and extension of the present. The future does not constitute an unknown and unknowable time or space—one too different to be imagined and too distant to be breached. It instead serves as a defamiliarised version of the present that is intended to provide 'us' with a new vantage point from which to look back at ourselves. In the discourses of the ecomodernists, the future ultimately serves to recreate and reproduce the anthropocentric values, expectations and assumptions of the present, asserting their continued relevance by imagining their continued survival.

This is the critique that Clive Hamilton levels against the ecomodernist project and its 'commitment to a "second creation" by technological means.'[25] The supposed newness of the remade world of the ecomodernists is nothing more than a ruse because, as Hamilton argues, it is based on the dreams and aspirations of 'those who can only imagine a future as an enlarged version of the present.'[26] Writing under the banner of the Dark Mountain Project, John Michael Greer makes a similar point about most contemporary imaginings of future worlds: these futures are 'just like the present, only a little more so.'[27] Imagined futures, these thinkers suggest, serve as a 'painted screen'—a mirror—that simply reflects the present back at itself.[28] But, crucially, this critique can also be extended to the work of Hamilton himself and to the writings of the so-called mountaineers who seek to find 'new paths and new stories' to lead them to a supposedly new world. In their own diagnoses of the present and their visions of the future, these thinkers replicate the same future-retrospective gaze that Ellis employs, and, with it, they also similarly co-opt the future into a mere projection of the present. Hamilton imagines the 'new humans' of the future building a 'new civilization from the planetary ashes of the old one' so as to look back upon the remains of the old world and declare, 'Never again.'[29] Meanwhile, for the mountaineers, the journey human beings must take beyond the 'end of the world' into the much-welcomed 'uncivilised' future will entail 'look[ing] back' upon the metaphorical 'pinprick lights of the distant cities' of old, to 'gain perspective on who we are and what we have become.' The worlds that are envisaged here—worlds that supposedly exist hundreds of thousands of years from now, or that are, at least, supposed to remain 'hidden from view,' a 'long way across the plains [. . .] obscured by distance'[30]—serve as refuges for an anthropocentric gaze that remains rooted in the present, a gaze that asserts and affirms the significance of the present even when it appears to fundamentally denounce it.

Dismissing the belief in 'technological mastery' that guides ecomodernist thinkers and climate engineers, Hamilton calls for the emergence of a new form of humanity that would 'embody another future,' human beings who would 'allow themselves to be appropriated by the next future' rather than attempt to engineer future worlds to the specifications of the present.[31] In his envisaging of this 'second civilization' that would follow on our own—a 'resurrected humanity' that would rise up to 'build a new civilization'—Hamilton claims that this future 'is too far off and uncertain for it to have any bearing on our times.'[32] But what Hamilton does not see is that the speculative world of the future that he imagines is in fact about *nothing more* than the present: it functions as a specular device that reflects and reproduces the world of today. Underlying Hamilton's conception of a new world is a distinctly Christian narrative and a belief in salvation and redemption that signals how far his own conceptions of the future are dependent on the values, assumptions and narratives that he appears to reject. Hamilton denounces modernity's 'grand narrative' of progress that seeks 'ever-higher technological and material development,' yet he proposes an even grander narrative of human transcendence in which human beings finally 'achieve maturity,' realise their 'destiny' and find their 'purpose' upon the earth.[33] This might not be a narrative of economic and technological progress, but it is a story of *human progress* nevertheless. For all his talk of newness, the story of the future that Hamilton tells is an age-old tale of tragedy and subsequent possible redemption, of humanity reborn in the garb of a humbled hero, finally overcoming his tragic fate so as to rise once more to greatness.[34] Even in imagined scenarios where the human species does *not* survive, the continued survival of the legacy of humankind and of its resounding significance upon the earth and the universe are, for Hamilton, never in doubt. Although he readily accepts that human beings 'may disappear from the face of the earth in the foreseeable future,' he nonetheless maintains that even 'in a hundred million years' time' when an alien civilization comes to write 'the history of the Universe,' 'the earth will be known as the Planet of the Humans.'[35] In Hamilton's assessment it is the presence of human beings upon the earth that grants the planet its 'cosmic significance,' and the continued memory and survival of this presence is guaranteed even in visions of the future in which human beings appear to be absent.[36]

A similar reliance on the past in the conceptualisation of a supposedly new world permeates the thought of the Dark Mountain Project. Like Hamilton, the mountaineers attack the myth of progress inherited from the Enlightenment, but they also seek to dismantle the notion of civilisation itself. In their manifesto for the project, Paul Kingsnorth and Dougald Hine reject the assumption that there is some kind of directionality to human history—that 'the future will be an upgraded version of the present' and 'that things must continue in their current direction.'[37] But they nevertheless situate the 'fall' of contemporary Western civilisation and the rise of the new 'uncivilised' world that they envisage within the general arc of human history—they present it as the latest in a long line of historical ascension and collapses that constitute 'a familiar human story.' 'That civilisations fall, sooner or later,' the manifesto claims, 'is as much a law of history as gravity is a law of physics.' It is now 'our civilisation's turn to experience the inrush of the savage and the unseen; our turn to be brought up short by contact with untamed reality.'[38] The coming end of Western civilisation is not conceived of here as the end of human history but as a distinctly *typical part* of it: as the working out, in fact, of its own natural law. That Kingsnorth and Hine describe the coming collapse using a rhetoric of 'savagery' and 'tameness' makes this even more evident: this rhetoric recalls the language of Western imperialism's civilising missions, and it creates an implicit parallel between the mountaineers' desire for *un*civilisation and the violence of the project of *civilisation* that they so forcefully renounce. While calling for the collapse of Western civilisation and all of its anthropocentric narratives, this manifesto continues to rely on the same tropes and motifs that sustain these myths, situating the supposedly 'uncivilised' future of a post-Anthropocene world within a continuum of shared human history.

This is further evidenced by Greer's contribution to the Dark Mountain Project.[39] Greer imagines the future 'rise and fall' of human societies repeating itself in accordance with 'the normal life cycle of civilisations.' He acknowledges that the deep future of the earth and of humanity cannot quite be imagined, but he anchors his inability to imagine this future in the certainty of the past. 'To judge by the evidence of history,' he asserts, 'each of those future societies will be as different from one another as they are from us, exploring realms of human possibility that, again, we can't even imagine today.'[40] The future may be unimaginable—but what is nevertheless certain for Greer is that *there will be* a future and that it will form part of a shared project of human history. Despite his dismissal of other futurologists who remain unable to escape the clutches of the present, Greer presents his readers with a vision of a post-Anthropocene world that is itself also rooted in the dominant narratives of the present and past. The repeated cycles of a rise and fall—of 'hubris and nemesis'—through which the manifesto reads the current crisis and in which Greer situates his own future worlds,[41] fit into what fellow mountaineer Chris Smaje identifies as the 'dualities of progress-regress, Eden-Fall, heaven-hell' produced by 'civilisation itself and its doctrines of modernisation.'[42] What is described in the manifesto and in Greer's writings as the natural 'law' and 'normal life cycle' of history[43] is actually one of the *founding narratives* of human civilisation—it is a paradigm through which human beings have repeatedly read and understood the present in relation to the past and the future. Rather than questioning the dominance of this paradigm, both texts replicate its logic, firmly situating their conceptualisations of the anthropocenic present and a post-anthropocenic future within the perspective of a shared human history that will extend beyond the collapse of any present world. Greer may very well discount the 'increasingly flimsy image' of the future that contemporary science-fiction narratives present us with, reflecting the present back to us under the guise of a future world.[44] But like Clive Hamilton's conceptualisation of a 'newborn *anthropos*,'[45] the Dark Mountain's own anthropocenic and post-anthropocenic narratives also function as mirrors of sorts, reflecting, replicating and projecting contemporary anthropocentric values and assumptions onto future worlds.

Whether they advocate a 'good' Anthropocene characterised by fantastical geoengineering projects, describe a 'bad' Anthropocene that should shock us out of our hubristic ways, or identify the present as the coming-of-age of a species that is of central importance to the earth and perhaps even the cosmos, each of these discourses is caught in a specular engagement with the future in which the post-Anthropocene functions as a continuation of the present, providing us with a means of reflection with which to contemplate the value and significance of our own world. In his descriptions of what he calls the 'technic societies of the deep future,' Greer argues that the future will not constitute a mere repetition of the present because future societies will have knowledge of our own present-day failures. Greer speculates that 'our fate will be discussed in hushed tones for centuries to come, and that this may provide a certain degree of immunisation against a repeat.'[46] For Greer, the very existence of the present will ensure that the future does not become a reflection or reproduction of the past. But what Greer does not seem to realise is that within the anthropocenic discourses he comments on and helps shape, the future *already* functions as such a reflection. His description of future human beings whispering in their post-anthropocenic societies about the unspeakable deeds of their ancestors is nothing more than a specular trope intended to redeem the present with the promise of a better future. The present *will have had value*, it *will have had significance*, it *will have had a purpose*, these speculations suggest, because, if nothing more, it will serve as the ultimate warning for a future humanity that will at long last be ready to mend its ways.

The future that is imagined in these discourses is one that *constitutes* the present: this is a future that *legitimises* and *validates* the present world, endowing it with historical significance, and it is a future that also *repeats* and *reproduces* the values and structures of the present, only, supposedly, better. Hamilton claims that 'in the Anthropocene we may say that the present is drenched with the future,' that our sense of the present is disturbed by 'the unsettling presence of times to come.'[47] But, equally, as I show here, the notion of the Anthropocene posits *a future that is drenched with the present*—a future that functions as a specular reflection of our own world and that will continue to be structured by the same discourses and practices of the present unless we find ways of reconceptualising our relationship to it. What is required is not more speculation about what the future may hold—more imagined future human beings and future worlds functioning as specular tropes for us to see ourselves in—but a reworking of some of the most fundamental concepts of the Anthropocene in a way that escapes the pull of their future-retrospective gaze. In the place of an anthropocentric gaze that looks at the earth but only ever sees the human, that looks to the future but only ever sees the present, what is required is a true rethinking of the world of the Anthropocene and the place that human beings hold within it.

Preserving the Present

In anthropocenic conceptualisations of the present as a future remnant of what once was, the current world functions as a spectral trace of itself—it constitutes an already-past, a fixed and indelible mark of something that survives in its own absence. This notion of spectrality is central to the whole logic of the Anthropocene: at its most basic level, this geological concept hinges on the belief that the mark of the human will be recorded forever in the earth's strata like some ghostly lithic signature that persists long after its signatories are gone. As Tobias Menely and Jesse Oak Taylor note, the anthropocenic trace marks a 'former presence' that 'endure[s]' in absence.[48] It is this spectrality that allows for the anthropocenic imaginary to postulate the future survival and persistence of the human, opening up a space of remembrance, mourning and redemption. To borrow from Derrida's discussion of 'the work of mourning' in *Specters of Marx*, the Anthropocene may be said to consist 'always in attempting to ontologize remains, to make them present.'[49] Projecting the present onto the future as a spectral trace of the past *ontologises* this future, rendering the current world present within it, allowing it to maintain its presence even in the face of its own absence. But while it allows the present to survive and persist beyond itself as a trace, the spectrality of the Anthropocene also *suspends* this same present, interrupting its existence as a lived and living state. If the present is already past, then it is already absent. The Anthropocene is conceptually predicated on a spectral interplay between these two points: it postulates a *presence* that persists and survives, but only in and as its own *absence*.

The effect of this spectral interplay is one of stasis. If the present is viewed or made to function as an already-past, then it becomes fixed, unchangeable and frozen in time. And if the future merely serves to mirror this suspended present, reproducing and repeating it in turn, then it is itself also similarly caught within this same static suspension. There is no room for change within this specular imaginary that only ever speculates *on itself*. Although as a cultural discourse the Anthropocene might masquerade as a harbinger of change, as creating what Bonneuil and Fressoz refer to as 'a new human condition' that makes possible a different kind of relationship with the earth,[50] this discourse is structured by a circular logic that forecloses the possibility for change, looping the present and future into a specular stasis of the self-same. This has serious implications for the way that the future is *conceptualised*, as well as the way that it is *constructed* through our discourses and practices. Having explored the workings of this specular logic in several discourses that attempt to make sense of the present world and envision other possible future versions of it, this chapter now turns its attention to a number of modern-day conservation practices that actively seek to *shape* the biological and material realities of the future. True to the spirit of the Anthropocene, projects like the Global Seed Vault,[51] or the Frozen Ark[52] and Frozen Zoo initiatives,[53] all seek to preserve and protect aspects of the present world for a future from which their archived contents might otherwise be absent. As I show in what follows, these projects exemplify and embody the archival logic of preservation that is implicit in the anthropocenic imaginary, and they open up the space for an exploration of the implications of this logic for the future. My analysis of these conservation projects serves a twofold purpose: on the one hand, it continues to show how the logic of future-retro-vision that lies at the heart of the Anthropocene reproduces and projects the anthropocentric values and assumptions of the present onto the future, shaping that future in a way that forecloses the possibility for change. On the other hand, it also points to the possibility of developing *other* ways of engaging with the notion of the Anthropocene and the spectral play of absence and presence that it hinges upon. As I show in what follows, a reconceptualisation of the very notion of spectrality can open the way for a revaluation of notions of human and non-human life and matter in the Anthropocene and allow for a rethinking of the values and assumptions that structure the current world and its anthropocentric discourses and practices.

The Global Seed Vault in Svalbard, Norway, the Frozen Ark initiative in the UK, and the Frozen Zoo project in San Diego in the US all seek to combat future species extinction and biodiversity loss by preserving seeds, embryos and the DNA and tissue samples of different living species with the aim of saving them for posterity. These conservation initiatives do not merely work to *prevent* the extinction of species or the loss of specific populations of animals and plants; they are designed to ensure the possibility of a *revival* and *repopulation* of species in the face of future loss. These projects use varying methods of preservation—from the naturally occurring low temperatures of the Arctic Circle to cryogenic freezing—but they all operate in the same spectral way: they interrupt the biological functioning of living cells, suspending them in a state of *deanimation* with the aim of reanimating and reviving them at a future time.[54] Located deep in the mountains of the Norwegian islands of Svalbard, the seed bank stores seeds from over a million crop species from around the world, serving as an 'insurance policy' or even a 'final back up' for the world's food supplies.[55] Meanwhile, the Frozen Ark—an international consortium of different conservation projects and initiatives—seeks to 'collect, preserve and conserve tissue, gametes, viable cells, and DNA of animal species facing extinction,'[56] and the Frozen Zoo aims to create 'a worldwide legacy of irreplaceable reproductive and genetic material that can be used in support of species conservation.'[57] As Sophia Roosth notes in a discussion of the Svalbard seed bank, these facilities all contain 'artifacts of the *present* [. . .] buried for *future* disinterral';[58] they function as bridges to the future, preserving the world's current biological heritage for decades and centuries to come, with the hopes of allowing it to be reseeded and revived at a later time.

These projects are all animated by a similar sense of future-retrospectivity to that which structures the notion of the Anthropocene. This future-retro-vision is necessitated by the structure of the archive itself that always derives its significance from a position of speculative futurity. Derrida tells us that 'if we want to know what [the archive] *will have meant*, we will only know in times to come.'[59] This is true of the seed vaults and biobanks we are considering here: these projects preserve aspects of the present world for the future in the hopes that they will one day be reanimated and revived. And it is precisely from within the space of this projected future that they derive their value. It is only when the seeds and biological specimens they contain are brought back to life—when they are resurrected in the future as living remnants of the past—that these archives will have achieved their purpose. The contents of these vaults have value because, in the future, they are *that which will have been archived, that which will have been preserved* and *that which will have been saved*. As Jonny Bunning explains in a discussion of human cryonics, such practices of preservation constitute 'a speculative "pro-ject," a throwing forward' that, it is hoped, will retrospectively legitimate the present.[60] The logic of speculative futurity creates 'a justificatory schema that runs back from the future, not forward from the present,' and the dominant tense here 'is not the simple future, but future perfect.'[61] At their very core, these preservation projects are thus structured by the same future-retrospec-tivity that animates the Anthropocene: a logic by which the present is made to function as a future relic of itself, and in which the actions and desires of the present are legitimated and redeemed in the projected ambitions of a speculative future.

Indeed, Deborah Bird Rose diagnoses in the practices of cryonic science the same redemptive logic that permeates the discourses of the Anthropo-cene. These technologies 'raise enticing possibilities of continuity across disaster and into some future, more welcoming world,' and in the narratives that structure them 'the linearity of time that is oriented toward the end [. . .] becomes complicated by the idea that when the end arrives, it will wash back over the time that preceded it, and remake this time.'[62] As in the anthropocenic imaginary, the archival logic behind these seed vaults and biobanks is predicated on the possibility of some future human redemption, on the hope that the anthropocentric world of the present will be given value and meaning—that it will be granted existence, even—through its survival into the future. Of course, these seed vaults and biobanks are explicitly intended to protect and preserve *non-human* life, but in truth the legacy and future that they are designed to secure is that of a *human* world. The purpose of the Svalbard repository is to collect and preserve the seeds of crops that are 'consumed by humans or as feed to farmed animals,'[63] while the Frozen Ark counts as some of its central aims the need to ensure that 'the beauty, splendour and practical solutions found in all species' can be 'noted and used by man,' and that the 'genetic material of endangered animals' can be conserved 'for the benefit of [presumably human] future generations.'[64] What is preserved and protected by these facilities is not merely non-human life but a certain understanding of what non-human life is, how it relates to human beings and why it has value. As Ursula Heise argues in her discussion of the unintentional biases that structure many conservation projects, 'biodiversity, endangered species, and extinction are primarily cultural issues, questions of what we value and what stories we tell.'[65] These projects may indeed arise out of a well-intentioned desire to create a more sustainable future for all, humans and non-humans alike, but they are nevertheless structured according to a redemptive anthropocentric logic that seeks to reproduce and replicate a particular version of the present into the future, validating and legitimising it retrospectively through its own speculative hopes of survival.

Like any other archive, these seed vaults and biobanks do not simply preserve the biological contents of their vaults. Through the very logic and structure of their archival gestures, they also reproduce the assumptions, values, discourses and practices by which this content is preserved, understood and granted significance. Along with their declared cargo of seeds and tissue samples, these so-called arks[66] also smuggle into the future very specific sets of scientific and cultural beliefs and practices that determine how life is conceptualised and categorised, how it is preserved, what value and function it is given and how it can be put to use. This is evident in the way that these facilities categorise and preserve their contents, treating 'life' as something that can be extracted out of its lived ecological realities and preserved as an autonomous and isolatable entity. Discussing the Svalbard seed bank and the Frozen Zoo initiative, Thom van Dooren explains that these projects sacrifice individual organisms for 'that most cherished strata of biodiversity, the species,' and they necessarily also disregard the rich interspecies assemblages and ecological realities within which these organisms live.[67] Frozen samples and specimens are valued for the genetic legacy they appear to hold—the legacy of a particular *species*, perceived as an independent, self-contained, self-reproducing unit of information that can be, both conceptually and in practice, isolated from any wider ecosystem, habitat or assemblage. As Matthew Chrulew also argues, the 'salvific suspension' that is practiced by these projects 'is only achieved by separating a secured element of the species from the relational context of animals' lives—their emplacement and duration, their phenomenological worlding, their political, cultural, and ecological milieus.'[68] These projects do not simply preserve 'life'—they preserve a specific form of life, and, with it, a specific understanding of what life is: one in which 'corporeal living beings' are perceived 'less as subjects of worlds in evolving community than as expressions of code, temporary vessels of information.'[69]

What is preserved in these arks and projected into the future is not simply the 'life' of a non-human species but a particular version of it—a product that has been shaped and formed by contemporary scientific practices and cultural discourses that reveal themselves to be broadly dependent on liberal humanist notions of autonomy, independence and self-sufficiency reductively applied and extended to the entirety of the living world. These projects thus reproduce and replicate at once *far more* and *far less* than the lifeforms they seek to preserve: through their practices of sample selection and preservation, they replicate a set of deeply ingrained beliefs about the value, purpose and nature of human and non-human life, and they project these values onto the future, allowing for a very specific kind of 'life' to emerge out of their vaults. In their efforts to freeze, halt and then revive, reseed and reestablish the present, these projects reduce complex lived ecological realities into spectral traces of suspended life, and through the very structure of their archival logic they reproduce a distinctly anthropocentric understanding of the purpose and functioning of living beings. If the world of the future were to be truly born from these arks, then it would be a world shaped *by* and *for* the human, one that would be structured by the same techno-futurist and capitalist hopes and desires that created the need for environmental salvation and redemption in the first place.

The world that is envisaged by such projects is one that can only truly survive *as it is now*. These conservation projects all work by preserving life in the present, suspending its processes and freezing it in place, precluding it from any further growth or transformation. The notion of preservation is predicated on the ability to seemingly halt the passage of time and create a state of immutable suspension through which the present can be carried into the future untouched and unscathed. The risk that is run here is that the very attempt to preserve and protect the present for the future will be what arrests the possibility for much-needed change. As Joanna Radin and Emma Kowal explain, 'the promise of an ever-receding and technoscientifically enabled, horizon of future salvation' can lead to an 'abdication of responsibility for action in the present,' and 'the instinct to defer and preserve' can itself be 'an impediment to an actually sustainable future brought about through decisive action and accountability.'[70] The desire to reseed the future—to freeze and then revive remnants of the present at a time in which they have become past—constitutes an attempt to both *suspend* the present into a spectral trace of itself and to specularly *reproduce* it in the future. As Deborah Bird Rose notes, it constitutes an attempt to skip over years of possible biological and cultural change and transformation, 'stopping, kick-starting, or leaping across time,'[71] so as to reanimate the present in the place of possibly radically other futures. The archival gestures that dominate these conservation efforts are distinctly anthropocentric and anthropocenic in their understanding of what might constitute a future world, and they perpetuate a circular logic by means of which the present is lived in anticipation of a future that remains in itself a specular projection of this same present.

Of course, many of the conservation efforts being discussed here—these modern-day arks stocked with frozen seeds, DNA and tissue samples—*are* explicitly intended to protect life on earth from one possible version of a radically other future: that of widespread extinction and irreparable biodiversity loss. Such projects often constitute last-ditch attempts to protect species that will otherwise go extinct, and in this respect their aims are infinitely laudable. But one must tread carefully here, for the very desire to protect and preserve non-human life in the present can itself be what forecloses the possibility of a future that is no longer structured by the same kinds of Western anthropocentric principles and assumptions that have, over the past centuries, fuelled the destruction of natural habitats and species. Going forward, what is needed is not a self-perpetuating reproduction of the cultural and scientific discourses and practices that structure our own world, but a thorough re-evaluation of some of the foundations beneath them. Commenting on the wider relevance of the politics of cryobiology to contemporary discussions about the Anthropocene, Radin and Kowal advocate redirecting 'attention away from anxieties about the future to examine the assumptions that guide actions in the present.'[72] One way of doing this, they argue, is by being attentive to what the effort to preserve life reveals about 'Western hierarchies of life' and its strict 'borders between life and death, human and nonhuman, self and other, past and future, animate and inanimate.'[73] It is only by probing and problematising the parameters of these seemingly self-evident oppositions—oppositions that have over the course of human history been used to determine what is of value and what is expendable, what ought to be protected and what can be erased—that we can begin to find alternative ways of living and thinking our present realities.

Rethinking Spectrality

One of the most foundational oppositions in the history of Western thought is that between the animate and the inanimate, with 'life' and the 'living' (often as generalised, abstract categories) being valorised and given priority over the perceived inertness of non-living matter. As Mel Chen notes, this opposition is intimately related to that between the human and the non-human[74]—an opposition that is at once more specific in what it gives value to and broader in what it leaves undefined. Through a hyponymic slippage that grants human beings more animacy, and therefore more 'life,' than any other non-human but possibly equally living entity, the value attributed to *life* functions as an extension of the higher value attributed to *human life*, confirming an anthropocentric bias that allows for non-human lifeforms to be objectified and commodified as non-living matter is. And within these 'brutal hierarchies of sentience,'[75] there exist many other distinctions, oppositions and slippages that grant higher value not merely to *human* life but, more specifically, to *certain kinds of human life*. These are not value-neutral distinctions that serve to innocently differentiate between one form of matter and another, or between certain kinds of life and those of others; these oppositions are structured according to a racialised anthropocentric logic by which 'some privileged humans are granted the status of thinking subject,'[76] and many other forms of human and non-human life, and living and non-living entities, are exploited as mere resources and commodities. Kathryn Yusoff argues that these hierarchies and oppositions underlie the discourses and practices that built the world of the Anthropocene—a world of climate and environmental crises and deep socio-economic injustices in which human beings and other species continue to be dehumanised, objectified and commodified together with the supposedly inanimate and eminently exploitable earth. Yusoff describes a 'contact point of geographical proximity [. . .] constructed specifically as a node of extraction of properties and personhood' by which natural environments and human and non-human beings are treated as an 'inhuman' resource that can be appropriated, exploited and effaced at will by those who have granted themselves the position, the privilege and the power to do so.[77] The opposition between life and non-life—between the animate and the inanimate, the lively and the inert—is thus intimately aligned 'with concepts of the human and inhuman' in ways that facilitate 'the divisions between subjects as humans and subjects priced as flesh (or inhuman matter).'[78] These oppositions work together to delineate, categorise and stratify different forms of human and non-human life and matter in accordance with biocentric, anthropocentric and racialised structures of power that value *life*, *human life* and, more specifically, a particular *form of human life*, over any other kind of living or material existence.

The overlapping of these oppositions and categories means that our efforts to question and challenge the anthropocentrism of the Anthropocene must not merely problematise and revalorise the distinction between the human and the non-human and all the racialised stratifications that this distinction involves; it must also further question and explore the opposition between the animate and the inanimate. As Yusoff notes, what is needed is 'to move beyond the narrow terrain of the biopolitical and "life itself" as the organizing concept for planetary existence' and to 'reorganize our understanding of human life'—and, I would add, *life* more broadly—'as located in a larger field of materiality.'[79] Rather than continue to conceptualise the Anthropocene through an anthropocentric gaze that assesses the world according to the relative presence or absence of a valued 'human' life within it, we must attempt to reconceptualise all of human existence as part of a much broader and richer inter-relationality of different forms of life and matter so as to challenge our very understanding of what has value and what does not. Released from its future-retrospective gaze, the notion of the Anthropocene can be reconceptualised to reveal the materiality of the human and other forms of biological existence, showing us that living beings are never 'exclusively biological'[80] and that the strict divisions between life and matter on which the supremacy of the 'human' has been predicated—the 'human' as the epitome of life, of living presence and of survival—can and should be breached. Rather than engaging with specular visions of ourselves projected into the future, we ought to consider the materiality of our existence *now*. As Yusoff rightly notes, this will entail 'taking up the (inhumanist) space that is opened by the concept [of the Anthropocene] while refuting the basic architectures of thought that structure that space (where humanity is used as a term of erasure of material and political forms of differentiation).'[81]

One way of broaching this conceptual space is through a reconceptualisation of the spectrality of the Anthropocene—a rereading of how and why the anthropocenic present might be said to be spectral. We can take as an example the spectral states of cryobiosis used by the archival biobanks to preserve their biological contents. As Sophia Roost notes, the contents of these archives can be thought of as 'self-referential material apparatuses manifesting theories of what life is, what it is not, and what lies in between'[82]—states of organic matter that can allow us to problematise the strict division between the living and the non-living and, consequently, help us to rethink the notions of presence and absence as they manifest themselves in thought about the Anthropocene. Within the anthropocenic imaginary that animates these projects, these frozen seeds and specimens are viewed and treated as *living* entities—as examples of a life that has been paused, awaiting its own return. The expressed aim of these facilities is to protect, preserve and extend life, and although their frozen contents display no *actual* signs of life, this absence is perceived and treated as a spectral precursor to the living presence that, it is believed, will one day reawaken out of these vaults. In this sense, these conservation projects are structured by the same logic that animates the practices of *human* cryopreservation in which vitrified bodies are referred to and treated as 'patients' rather than dead corpses because their present state of deanimation is viewed retrospectively through the lens of a future in which they may be revived.[83] Within the archival logic that permeates the cryonic imaginary and that underlies much of our thinking of the Anthropocene, absence is ontologised into a presence that promises to return. As I have shown, the present may appear absent to itself, but this absence is vindicated through the continued promise of survival—the survival of the memory and legacy of the human in the Anthropocene, or the survival and reanimation of these frozen lives in some supposedly unknown future. But this spectral interplay of presence and absence need not be viewed in this way. The spectrality that animates (or, better still, *deanimates*) the logic of these discourses and practices can be understood *hauntologically* rather than *ontologically*,[84] in a way that problematises the distinction between absence and presence and puts into question the valorisation of *living* presence (and, above all, lived *human* presence) over every other form of material existence.

Discussing the state of 'latent life' in which the frozen and cryopreserved contents of these archives are held, Radin and Kowal note that this constitutes a 'liminal and vague state between life and death,'[85] one that interrupts the molecular processes by which life grows, reproduces, evolves, survives, decays and even dies. These suspended states of cryonic freezing *deanimate* living tissue in a manner that is not simply akin to death, because, like life, death involves the ongoing transformation and recomposition of biological matter.[86] These states of preservation in which nothing truly lives, nothing truly dies and nothing seems to change are more comparable to the supposedly inert states of non-living matter that we routinely oppose lived existence to.[87] If, as Sophia Roost notes, 'latently living things' can only be 'identified according to their *potential future life* or are recognized in *retrospect* only *after* they revive,' this is because in their present dormant, latent, cryosuspended or frozen state, they function as forms of seemingly inert matter—material '*things*'—that are not actually alive in any simple or straightforward way.[88] For Roosth, this reveals a porous interchange, rather than an opposition, between the living and the non-living—between supposedly animate life and inanimate matter. These examples of suspended or latent life show that life can be discontinuous and reversible, that the living can become inert in ways that go beyond mere death, that what appears as non-living can always turn out to be alive and that the relationship between lived existence and material persistence is fluid, transmutable and complex. Viewed in this way, life cannot simply be thought of as a form of *presence*—as that which exists in and of itself and is active and animate. And matter cannot simply be viewed as constituting an inert state of *absence*—one that is not alive and cannot animate itself. The two become implicated in one another, revealing the possible animacy of supposedly inanimate matter and the inanimacy of life, in an interdependency that annuls any simple distinction between presence and absence.

This notion of interdependence becomes even more complex if one considers how states of latency are created and maintained by particular environmental conditions. The very idea of an 'environment' is somewhat problematic here, because of course the term implies a life, a being or a presence that is *surrounded* by a world. But latent life is not merely *surrounded* by an environment; it is patently *produced* by it. It is the materiality of ice and the cold temperatures of the glacier-fitted vaults that suspend biological processes of growth, reproduction, germination, death and decay—both in the case of the seed samples held in Svalbard and in many other kinds of latent life (such as bacterial spores or viruses that lie buried and frozen in the Arctic).[89] The continued existence of such deanimated biological matter is entirely dependent on these supposedly 'external' environmental factors, and any possible reanimation of these spores and seeds will likewise also be entirely contingent on changes in these conditions. The same is true of the DNA and tissue samples stored in the so-called frozen zoos and arks, and of the hundreds of vitrified human bodies and heads held in cryopreservation facilities around the world. While, as Richard Doyle notes, 'nothing would seem so clearly isolated and autonomous as the cryonic body,' these bodies remain 'reliant on a whole swarm of others for [their] maintenance and [their] promise of revival.'[90] The states of latency in which this biological matter continues to exist are materially produced by the solutions of liquid nitrogen within which this matter is immersed, and they remain more broadly dependent on the complex scientific, technological, economic and environmental realities that make such processes of preservation both possible and desirable. These examples of latent deanimated life thus do not merely blur the boundaries between the animate and the inanimate—between the supposed presence of animate life and its absence in inanimate matter. They also reveal how these supposed states of presence and absence are themselves always entangled in complex interdependent webs and networks of material, biological and discursive phenomena in which nothing can ever be said to be truly present or absent to itself because such presence is only ever constituted through otherness.

While practices of cryopreservation are, as we have seen, predicated on the assumption that life is autonomous and isolatable and that it can be extracted out of its lived environment so as to be preserved *ex-situ*, the continued dependence of preserved biological matter on the environments with and within which it exists reveals that life is *never* extractable from its environment—not even in its supposedly most singular and isolatable state. Commenting on the example of human cryopreservation, Franziska von Verschuer describes this practice as an attempt by human beings to escape and negate the biological embeddedness of nature, to extract and insulate themselves from 'the relationality of all life.'[91] Von Verschuer diagnoses in this 'secular humanist [. . .] partially modernist, rationalist and male-dominated endeavour' a desire for the '*dezoefication*' of the human—for human beings to be disentangled from the collective workings and processes of the natural world by circumventing the 'material implications of being buried and disintegrated by worms and mould.'[92] What cryonic enthusiasts seek to avoid above all is 'the prospect of being merged into the sphere of Nature.'[93] But, of course, what they do not or cannot see is that life is *always* merged in the sphere of nature. Even in this supposedly supremely isolated and insulated state of cryopreservation—where a body is protected from any changes brought about by the ongoing processes of biological life—biological matter remains dependent on external conditions for its continued survival. Cryopreservation *itself* requires a host of material and technological processes that render the deanimated body reliant on 'external' material support. Cryopreservation does not produce a self-contained, isolatable and autonomous entity—it merely replaces the rich material interactivity and interdependency of biological life and death with a technologically mediated but equally dependent state of deanimation. While these practices may, to varying degrees, be modelled on an understanding of life that treats the living subject as individual, autonomous and self-present, what they reveal is an entanglement of life and death, the animate and the inanimate, the biological and the non-biological—an entanglement by which life is always embedded in other living and material states.

If these frozen and cryopreserved entities are spectral, then it is not merely because they are not fully alive, or because they are not fully dead; it is because their presence is always mediated through that which is supposedly external (and therefore 'non-present') to them. Whether alive or not, these seeds, samples and bodies are always dependent on and entangled in the supposedly external material conditions with and within which they continue to exist. According to Derrida, this is what 'all philosophies of life, or even philosophies of the living and real individual [. . .] have to weigh carefully'—that the spectre of the other (of the supposed absence of life, of the inanimate, of the material, of all that lies beyond the supposedly singular most autonomous organism) 'intensifies and condenses itself within the very inside of life, within the most living life, the most singular (or, if one prefers, individual) life.' Life, 'insofar as it is living,' Derrida asserts, 'no longer has and must no longer have [. . .] a pure identity to itself or any assured inside.'[94] To view life *hauntologically* is to view it in this way—*materially*—to acknowledge its embeddedness in that which supposedly lies outside of it, disrupting any simple notion of its own self-presence. And this is precisely what a hauntological reading of the spectrality of the Anthropocene can offer. Thinking the Anthropocene need not necessarily lead to an *ontologising* of the present—to the present being conceived through the lens of a future that redeems it through its own supposed absence. It need not mean getting caught between the possibility of imagining an anthropocentric future and the impossibility of imagining that which must remain unknown, and it need not be predicated on the relative presence or absence of a single isolated human gaze upon this world. What is needed is what Karen Barad describes as a 're-membering':[95] not an attempt to preserve and archive the present world in order for it to be recalled, reclaimed and remembered in the future, but an attempt to recognise the way that the present is itself always enfolded in otherness, always re-*membered* out of difference, always entangled in complex interweavings of biological and material phenomena that are 'spooky'[96] and spectral because they can never be simply present to themselves. To approach the notion of the Anthropocene in this way requires that one 'acknowledge and be responsive to the noncontemporaneity of the present,'[97] not by rerouting this present through the anthropocentric and redemptive lens of an imagined future but by accounting for the way in which it is always other to itself, always embedded in that which it supposedly is not. It is only by viewing ourselves and our own present as embedded in the material worlds and biological realities that we so often separate ourselves from that we can ever hope to find a way out of the Anthropocene echo-chamber.

Notes

1. Sverker Sörlin, "The Mirror—Testing the Counter-Anthropocene," in *Future Remains: A Cabinet of Curiosities for the Anthropocene*, ed. Gregg Mitman, Marco Armiero, and Robert S. Emmett (Chicago: University of Chicago Press, 2018), 171.

2. Joanna Zylinska, *The End of Man: A Feminist Counterapocalypse* (Minneapolis: University of Minnesota Press, 2018), 3.

3. Mary Louise Pratt, "Coda: Concept and Chronotope," in *Arts of Living on a Damaged Planet*, ed. Anna Tsing, Heather Swanson, Elaine Gan, and Nils Bubandt (Minneapolis: University of Minnesota Press, 2017), G170.

4. Tobias Menely and Jesse Oak Taylor, eds. *Anthropocene Reading: Literary History in Geologic Times* (University Park: Pennsylvania State University Press, 2017), 3.

5. Zylinska, *The End of Man*, 9–12.

6. Tom Cohen, Claire Colebrook, and J. Hillis Miller, *Twilight of the Anthropocene Idols* (London: Open Humanities Press, 2016), 86.

7. Bronislaw Szerszynski, "The End of the End of Nature: The Anthropocene and the Fate of the Human," *The Oxford Literary Review* 34, no. 2 (December 2012): 169, https://doi.org/10.3366/olr.2012.0040.

8. Szerszynski, "The End of the End of Nature," 180–81.

9. Noah Heringman, "The Anthropocene Reads Buffon; or, Reading Like Geology," in *Anthropocene Reading*. Menely and Taylor, 60–61.

10. Jan Zalasiewicz, *The Earth After Us: What Legacy Will Humans Leave in the Rocks?* (Oxford: Oxford University Press, 2008), 1.

11. Indeed, Zalasiewicz frames the possibility of humankind's survival in the strata as constituting a 'potential for immortality,' and he jokingly recommends that readers might take certain specific measures (as detailed in his own book) to 'increase [their] chances of carrying a final message, that of [their] own brief existence, into the next geological era' (Zalasiewicz, *The Earth After Us*, 3, 6).

12. Dipesh Chakrabarty, "The Climate of History: Four Theses," *Critical Inquiry* 35, no. 2 (Winter 2009): 198, https://doi.org/10.1086/596640.

13. Jacques Derrida, *Archive Fever: A Freudian Impression*, trans. Erin Prenowitz (Chicago: University of Chicago Press, 1996), 3.

14. Paul J. Crutzen and Eugene F. Stoermer, "The 'Anthropocene,'" *Global Change Newsletter* no. 41 (May 2000): 17.

15. Erle C. Ellis, "Neither Good nor Bad," *New York Times*, May 23, 2011, https://www.nytimes.com/roomfordebate/2011/05/19/the-age-of-anthropocene-should-we-worry/neither-good-nor-bad.

16. "An Ecomodernist Manifesto," April 2015, 7, http://www.ecomodernism.org.

17. Erle C. Ellis, "Planet of No Return: Human Resilience on an Artificial Earth," *Breakthrough Journal*, no. 2 (Fall 2011), https://thebreakthrough.org/journal/issue-2/the-planet-of-no-return.

18. "Ecomodernist Manifesto," 23–24.

19. "Ecomodernist Manifesto," 17.

20. Paul Kingsnorth and Dougald Hine, "Uncivilisation: The Dark Mountain Manifesto," The Dark Mountain Project, 2009, https://dark-mountain.net/about/manifesto/.

21. Clive Hamilton, *Defiant Earth: The Fate of Humans in the Anthropocene* (London: Polity, 2017), 67.

22. Hamilton, *Defiant Earth*, 9.

23. Hamilton, *Defiant Earth*, 63, 111.

24. Erle C. Ellis, "Forget Mother Nature: This Is a World of Our Making," *New Scientist*, June 8, 2011, https://www.newscientist.com/article/mg21028165-700-forget-mother-nature-this-is-a-world-of-our-making/.

25. Hamilton, *Defiant Earth*, 26–27.

26. Hamilton, *Defiant Earth*, 156.

27. John Michael Greer, "2016: Toward the Deep Future," The Dark Mountain Project, January 19, 2017, https://dark-mountain.net/2016-toward-the-deep-future/.

28. Greer, "2016: Toward the Deep Future."

29. Hamilton, *Defiant Earth*, 162.

30. Kingsnorth and Hine, "Dark Mountain Manifesto."

31. Hamilton, *Defiant Earth*, 156.

32. Hamilton, *Defiant Earth*, 162.

33. Hamilton, *Defiant Earth*, 117, 124.

34. Indeed, one of the images Hamilton uses to describe this new humanity is that of 'Shakespeare's man, both glorious and tragic, for whom human benevolence is what is at stake and the aspiration to omnipotence is the most dangerous temptation' (Hamilton, *Defiant Earth*, 126).

35. Hamilton, *Defiant Earth*, 115.

36. Hamilton, *Defiant Earth*, 116.

37. Kingsnorth and Hine, "Dark Mountain Manifesto."

38. Kingsnorth and Hine, "Dark Mountain Manifesto."

39. Greer, "2016: Toward the Deep Future."

40. Greer, "2016: Toward the Deep Future."

41. Kingsnorth and Hine, "Dark Mountain Manifesto."

42. Chris Smaje, "Dark Thoughts on Ecomodernism," The Dark Mountain Project, August 12, 2015, https://dark-mountain.net/dark-thoughts-on-ecomodernism-2/.

43. Kingsnorth and Hine, "Dark Mountain Manifesto"; Greer, "2016: Toward the Deep Future."

44. Greer, "2016: Toward the Deep Future."

45. Hamilton, *Defiant Earth*, 121.

46. Greer, "2016: Toward the Deep Future."

47. Hamilton, *Defiant Earth*, 132.

48. Menely and Taylor, *Anthropocene Reading*, 7.

49. Jacques Derrida, *Specters of Marx: The State of the Debt, the Work of Mourning, and the New International*, trans. Peggy Kamuf (New York: Routledge, 1994), 9.

50. Christophe Bonneuil and Jean-Baptiste Fressoz, *The Shock of the Anthropocene*, trans. David Fernbach (London: Verso, 2017), 20.

51. Svalbard Global Seed Vault, https://www.seedvault.no/.

52. Frozen Ark, https://www.frozenark.org/.

53. Frozen Zoo, San Diego Zoo Wildlife Alliance, https://science.sandiegozoo.org/resources/frozen-zoo%C2%AE.

54. The term 'deanimation' is primarily used by proponents of human cryopreservation to signal a state of lifelessness that, contrary to death, is neither irreversible nor final (Alcor, "A Brief Scientific Introduction to Cryonics," https://www.alcor.org/library/a-brief-scientific-introduction-to-cryonics/). My own use of this term is intended to draw attention to the way that cryopreserved matter exists in a state that belongs to neither *life* nor *death*. Indeed, as we shall see, preserved bodies, seeds and other biological materials are extracted out of the cycles of life and growth, decay and decomposition, and are preserved in what can be described as both a *lifeless* and a *deathless* form of stasis.

55. "Svalbard Global Seed Vault," Crop Trust, accessed June 16, 2021, https://www.croptrust.org/our-work/svalbard-global-seed-vault/.

56. "Our Vision, Mission Statement & Key Aims," The Frozen Ark, accessed June 16, 2021, https://www.frozenark.org/vision-and-mission-statement.

57. Frozen Zoo, San Diego Zoo Wildlife Alliance, accessed June 16, 2021, https://science.sandiegozoo.org/resources/frozen-zoo%C2%AE.

58. Sophia Roosth, "Virus, Coal, and Seed: Subcutaneous Life in the Polar North," *Los Angeles Review of Books*, December 21, 2016, https://lareviewofbooks.org/article/virus-coal-seed-subcutaneous-life-polar-north/.

59. Derrida, *Archive Fever*, 36; emphasis added.

60. Jonny Bunning, "The Freezer Program: Value After Life," in *Cryopolitics: Frozen Life in a Melting World*, ed. Joanna Radin and Emma Kowal (Cambridge, MA: MIT Press, 2017), 232.

61. Bunning, "Freezer Program," 219, 229.

62. Deborah Bird Rose, "Reflections on the Zone of the Incomplete," in *Cryopolitics*, Radin and Kowal, 146, 150.

63. "Seed Deposit 2020," 2020 Svalbard Seed Summit Press Package, Svalbard Global Seed Vault Deposit, February 25, 2020, https://www.regjeringen.no/globalassets/departementene/ud/vedlegg/nord/presskit_svalbard.pdf.

64. "About the Frozen Ark Project," The Frozen Ark, accessed February 2020, https://www.frozenark.org/.

65. Ursula K. Heise, *Imagining Extinction: The Cultural Meanings of Endangered Species* (Chicago: University of Chicago Press, 2016), 5.

66. The Svalbard Seed Bank is itself also often referred to as an 'ark' (see, for instance, Malia Wollan, "Arks of the Apocalypse," *New York Times Magazine*, July 13, 2017, https://www.nytimes.com/2017/07/13/magazine/seed-vault-extinction-banks

-arks-of-the-apocalypse.html; and Michael Day, "Noah's Ark for Plants to Store World's Seeds," *Telegraph*, January 28, 2008, https://www.telegraph.co.uk/news/ear th/earthnews/3323301/Noahs-Ark-for-plants-to-store-worlds-seeds.html). The image of the ark has a rich history within environmental discourse. Sabine Höhler argues that this biblical allusion lies at the root of the widely used image of 'Spaceship Earth'—the idea that the earth functions as a vessel for humanity, equipped with finite resources and a finite amount of space. 'At a moment when the earth was discovered as a paradise soon to be lost,' Höhler notes, 'the spaceship expressed the vision of a modern-day ark to preserve and extend earthly life by new means' (Sabine Höhler, *Spaceship Earth in the Environmental Age, 1960–1990* (London: Routledge, 2015), 22). Höhler links this image to imperial and colonial ideas of expansion, arguing that Western awareness over the confinement and limitations of the earth partly arose out of the exhaustiveness of colonial projects that mapped out and captured what were previously considered *terrae incognitae*, and she further argues that these discourses borrow their language from the 'science and technology of space flight in the visions to overcome earthly limits by eventually constructing biosphere surrogates and recovering living space elsewhere' (Höhler, *Spaceship Earth*, 5). The idea of imperial expansion extends nowadays to projects of space exploration and colonisation, where the notion of the ark features once more. The project known as 'Project Persephone,' for instance—conceptualised as 'a space programme for the rest of us' (http://www.projectpersephone.org/pmwiki/pmwiki.php)—has been described in the media as a 'space ark' that 'will save man from a dying planet' (Kaya Burgess, "Space Ark Will Save Man from a Dying Planet," *The Times*, April 28, 2014, https://www.thetimes.co.uk/article/space-ark-will-save-man-from-a-dying-planet-c0xh08vzsb2).

67. Thom van Dooren, "Banking the Forest: Loss, Hope, and Care in Hawaiian Conservation," in *Cryopolitics*, Radin and Kowal, 264.

68. Matthew Chrulew, "Freezing the Ark: The Cryopolitics of Endangered Species Preservation," in *Cryopolitics*, Radin and Kowal, 287.

69. Chrulew, "Freezing the Ark," 291–92. It is for this reason that Thom van Dooren argues that these projects function as more of a 'living tomb' than a vibrant 'ark.' Indeed, according to van Dooren, '[t]hat these projects are called "conservation" at all is itself deeply problematic,' as they separate a species from 'who it is—its evolved and evolving "way of life"—as well as much of what enables the species to survive in the wider world' (van Dooren, "Banking the Forest," 271–73).

70. Radin and Kowal, *Cryopolitics*, 9–10.

71. Rose, "Reflections," 146.

72. Radin and Kowal, *Cryopolitics*, 10.

73. Radin and Kowal, *Cryopolitics*, 17.

74. Mel Y. Chen, *Animacies: Biopolitics, Racial Mattering, and Queer Affect* (Durham, NC: Duke University Press, 2012), 29.

75. Chen, *Animacies*, 43.

76. Chen, *Animacies*, 43.

77. Kathryn Yusoff, *A Billion Black Anthropocenes or None* (Minneapolis: University of Minnesota Press, 2018), xii.

78. Yusoff, *Billion Black Anthropocenes*, 9.

79. Kathryn Yusoff, "Anthropogenesis: Origins and Endings in the Anthropocene," *Theory, Culture & Society* 33, no. 2 (March 2016): 9–10, https://doi.org/10.1177/0263276415581021.

80. Yusoff, "Anthropogenesis," 5.

81. Yusoff, "Anthropogenesis," 9.

82. Sophia Roosth, "Life, Not Itself: Inanimacy and the Limits of Biology," *Grey Room* 57 (Fall 2014): 75, https://doi.org/10.1162/GREY_a_00156.

83. Bunning, "Freezer Program," 232.

84. The term comes from Derrida, who distinguishes, in *Specters of Marx*, between an ontology based on a logic of presence and the *hauntological*—or a 'logic of haunting.' 'This logic of haunting," Derrida notes, 'would not be merely larger and more powerful than an ontology or a thinking of Being (of the "to be," [. . .]). It would harbour within itself, but like circumscribed places or particular effects, eschatology and teleology themselves' (Derrida, *Specters*, 10).

85. Radin and Kowal, *Cryopolitics*, 8.

86. This basic principle forms the basis of my discussion of *survivance* in Chapter 3, where I explore how movements of decomposition and recomposition are inherent to life but also extend beyond the living to non-living matter.

87. As I show in the following chapters, the idea that matter is inert is problematic. Matter may not appear to be animate, but perceived in its chemical states it remains reactive: it is able to decompose, transform into new states and interact with other products. As Diana Coole and Samantha Frost put it, matter is 'constantly forming and reforming in unexpected ways,' 'assembling and disintegrating' in 'choreographies of becoming' that extend across the living and the material world (Diana Coole and Samantha Frost, eds., *New Materialisms: Ontology, Agency, and Politics* (Durham, NC: Duke University Press, 2010), 10).

88. Roosth, "Life, Not Itself," 64, 74–75; emphasis added.

89. For more on this see Roosth, "Virus, Coal, and Seed."

90. Richard Doyle, *Wetwares: Experiments in Postvital Living* (Minneapolis: University of Minnesota Press, 2003), 62–63.

91. Franziska von Verschuer, "Freezing Lives, Preserving Humanism: Cryonics and the Promise of *Dezoefication*," *Distinktion: Journal of Social Theory* 21, no. 2 (April 2019): 144, https://doi.org/10.1080/1600910X.2019.1610016.

92. Von Verschuer, "Freezing Lives," 144.

93. Von Verschuer, "Freezing Lives," 151.

94. Derrida, *Specters*, 109.

95. Karen Barad, "Troubling Time/s and Ecologies of Nothingness: Re-turning, Re-membering, and Facing the Incalculable," *New Formations: A Journal of Culture/Theory/Politics* 92 (2018): 63, https://doi.org/10.3898/NEWF:92.05.2017; and Karen

Barad, "After the End of the World: Entangled Nuclear Colonialisms, Matters of Force, and the Material Force of Justice," *Theory & Event* 22, no. 3 (July 2019): 539.

96. Karen Barad, "Quantum Entanglements and Hauntological Relations of Inheritance: Dis/continuities, SpaceTime Enfoldings, and Justice-to-Come," *Derrida Today* 3, no. 2 (November 2010): 249, https://doi.org/10.3366/E1754850010000813.

97. Barad, "Quantum Entanglements," 264–65.

CHAPTER TWO

~

Lithic Textuality

Reading and Writing
Beyond Life and the Human

The concept of the Anthropocene is inherently semiotic: it is based on the assumption that geochemical phenomena in the earth's strata can function as signs that have meaning. In fact, one of the principle ideas underpinning the notion of the Anthropocene is that of a human 'signature' being inscribed in the earth.[1] Proponents of the term postulate that recent human activity has left a readable mark in the earth's crust, an unintentional 'we were here' that will remain legible for many millions of years. The notion of such an inscription derives from geology—a discipline that has long viewed the surface of the earth as an archival record, or even a 'stone book,' inscribed with the traces of past geological events.[2] In the branch of geology known as stratigraphy, scientists study how specific geochemical and biochemical materials deposited in sedimentary layers of rock thousands upon thousands of years ago can be used to identify changes and shifts in the earth's history. These materials are viewed and treated as signs that point to the occurrence of significant past geological events, allowing scientists to designate one geological period as being distinct from another.[3] As the geologist Jan Zalasiewicz explains, 'the layering of rocks [. . .] captures within itself [. . .] almost infinite possibilities for encapsulating stories of past landscapes,' allowing the earth's crust to function as a collection of 'stratal archives' encoded with 'signals' of the past.[4]

The notion of the Anthropocene emerges out of this tradition. As Tobias Menely and Jesse Oak Taylor note, the concept's viability is 'premised on a [. . .] narrowly semiotic claim about the clarity of a "signature" recorded in a lithostratigraphic archive' and on specific 'semiotic criteria' that determine what the nature of this signature might be.[5] Certain geochemical materials recently deposited in rock sediments—most notably, radionuclides from the testing of nuclear weapons in the second half of the twentieth century[6]—are believed to constitute a strong enough mark to signal the existence of a new epoch characterised by intense human activity on the planet. This mark, it is believed, will remain legible in the rocks for hundreds of thousands or even millions of years, continuing to bear witness to the human world of the present.

The Anthropocene is all about reading and writing. The scientific practices out of which this concept emerges are concerned with the identification and deciphering of lithic signs, and the notion of the Anthropocene is itself predicated on the assumption that the 'inscriptions' and 'signatures' being made in the strata of the earth by human beings will be readable in the future. As various commentators have noted, the Anthropocene is 'not simply something that is written *about*' but something that is *itself* written,[7] and it is not merely something that we read about but something that can itself also be read.[8] As Zalasiewicz describes it, the Anthropocene constitutes an epoch of anthropogenic changes that are represented in 'signposts,' 'traces' and 'mark[s]' 'written in the strata'—'message[s]' that have been unintentionally left behind for posterity.[9] The earth no longer functions merely as a 'stone book' that can be studied by geologists; it is now a book that can be *written by human beings* themselves.[10] The earth serves as both a history book that holds within it the secrets of the past, as well as a 'collective writing pad' that continues to record the anthropocenic activities of the present.[11]

But if the earth functions as a book, and the geochemical traces in its strata serve as signs or messages, then the question that must be asked here is: *For whom?* Who do these traces function as signs or messages for? This may seem like a banal question: these geochemical phenomena, one could easily respond, function as messages, signs or signals only insofar as they can be 'read' from within a particular human framework. Like any other sign, these marks exist *as signs* because they are recognised as such by those who read and interpret them. It seems obvious enough that outside of these interpretative frameworks—outside of the disciplines of geology and stratigraphy and other scientific and cultural practices and discourses—these geochemical phenomena would have no real meaning. With no trained human eye to read them, they would constitute a *difference* in the strata, certainly, but one that would have no particular semiotic value.

This seems straightforward enough. Discussing the way that Martian strata can be read in a similar manner to the stratigraphic reading of the earth,

Zalasiewicz suggests that the stories told by these rocks might be specific 'to current human eyes'[12]—that different ways of reading might result in a different tale, therefore, or, even, that there might be no tale at all without human beings to read it. But if it is human reading that makes the sign—if these stratigraphic marks only function as textual inscriptions insofar as they can be read by the human—then what are we to make of recent claims by ecocritics and theorists that there might be something *inherently textual* about the earth itself? Benjamin Morgan notes that the earth's rocks are engaged in a 'nonhuman production of meaning' that dramatises 'the capacity of nonhuman agencies to construct meaningful scales';[13] Jeffrey Cohen describes how the chemical elements that make up the earth can create 'open never-ended archives, labyrinthine libraries of the not-quite-read';[14] and Serenella Iovino and Serpil Oppermann suggest that 'there is an implicit textuality in the becoming of material formations, and this textuality resides in the way the agentic dimension of matter expresses itself.'[15] Meanwhile, Claire Colebrook argues that one of the real challenges of the Anthropocene is to be able to 'imagine a world without organic perception, without the centred points of view of sensing and world-oriented beings' by which human beings read and give meaning to their environments. For Colebrook, '*this would not be a world without reading*'; it would be one in which 'reading would take a radically different form.'[16] What could such a reading consist of? And why might it be necessary to speak of reading and writing in this way, as some movement of textuality that does not simply exist for the human?

The notion of a human anthropocenic inscription (of an inscription *made* by the human that can also be *read* by the human) underwrites the future-retrospective gaze of the Anthropocene. Inherent to the notion of the Anthropocene is the assumption that these lithic signs will be able to be deciphered in the future by the same kinds of stratigraphic systems of meaning by which scientists currently 'read' the past. The legibility of the anthropocenic sign is necessarily a *human* form of legibility that presupposes the continued existence of an anthropomorphic reader.[17] It is for this reason that the idea of the Anthropocene invites a future-retrospective gaze that anthropomorphises and co-opts the future, postulating the continued survival of the human even beyond its own collective death and extinction. If the Anthropocene is predicated on the notion of a sign that remains legible in the strata, and if signs only ever exist semiotically and within human frames of reference, then the notion of an anthropocenic inscription or signature automatically also posits the existence of a future anthropomorphic gaze that is able to read it. But what would happen if we were to challenge one of the basic principles on which these assumptions are founded: the idea that a lithic 'inscription' or 'trace' should be understood solely in terms of a human sign that is legible and decipherable within a human semiotic framework? What if we were to adapt our thinking of the trace and question our understanding of what constitutes textual inscription so as to explore the possibility of a lithic textuality that is not simply tied to human forms of representation and interpretation? How might this transform our understanding of the Anthropocene and related notions of presence and survival? This chapter explores the possibility of such thought, proposing an understanding of textuality that is not predicated on the continued presence or absence of the human, whether as producer, receiver or referent of the anthropocenic sign.

Metaphor, Meaning and Matter

It would be easy to relegate the notion of lithic inscription to the realm of mere metaphor. Discussing the widespread use of linguistic and textual analogies in geology, Bronislaw Szerszynski notes that the Victorian geologist David Thomas Ansted would probably be the first to declare that his own notion of 'the great stone book of nature' was nothing more than a 'fanciful metaphor.'[18] That the earth is only *metaphorically* textual seems obvious enough: the anthropocenic 'signatures' from radionuclide deposits in the earth's strata do not *literally* constitute a form of writing, and human beings do not use nuclear materials to engrave their names into the earth's strata. Stratigraphers track the presence of chemicals, minerals and fossils in the rocks, not letters and words. When geologists 'read' a stratigraphic trace, it is not a linguistic sign that they cast their eyes upon but a marked chemical difference in the strata. These differences can *function* as signs, certainly, within the interpretative frameworks that human beings bring to bear upon them— they can be read and interpreted in a manner that is *analogous* to the reading of a text—but they are not linguistic or textual entities in and of themselves. Although these traces often constitute chemical remnants of past events that can be said to point to the existence of something outside of themselves, this referentiality exists only insofar as it can be tracked down and interpreted by scientists. Outside of these human frameworks and systems of meaning, these traces constitute mere material phenomena devoid of any semiotic value. Understood in this way, the description of the earth as a textual surface inscribed with signs of the human may be viewed as a metaphor that represents the way that geologists and stratigraphers themselves approach, study and represent the earth—it is a metaphor that metonymically represents the way that the earth is itself represented and understood by its human observers.

Prod at these distinctions long enough, however, and they begin to unravel. Isn't it in the very nature of the sign to only act as a sign within a specific semiotic network? How is the lithic trace any different to a textual squiggle that only has meaning for the one who is able to decipher it? Wouldn't *every* sign be metaphorical, in a sense, if it referred to something outside of itself? And does an understanding of textuality necessarily have to be tied to the semiotic and the referential? Might there not be other, broader relationships between the textual and the lithic, the material and the discursive, metaphor and matter, that extend beyond human systems of meaning and reference and complicate the distinction between nature and culture as it is commonly understood? These questions tie in with some of the broader concerns that characterise recent new materialist thought in the humanities, and they invite us to take a closer look at the relationship between textuality, metaphoricity, meaning and matter so as to explore how a different understanding of the *textuality of the lithic*, and of matter more generally, might allow us to rethink some of the most basic anthropocentric assumptions that underlie the notion of the Anthropocene.

Such an exploration must begin with a consideration of the way that the relationship between language and reality has been most typically conceptualised in the history of Western thought. Karen Barad argues that the notion of human exceptionalism—the belief that human beings are somehow distinct from and superior to the rest of the natural world—has given rise to a representationalist worldview that posits language and other human systems of meaning as being fundamentally separate from so-called external reality.[19] As Barad describes it, 'representationalism is the belief in the ontological distinction between representations and that which they purport to represent,' and it is inherent to most conventional views of language, as well as many established philosophical and scientific discourses and practices.[20] Regardless of whether one subscribes to the traditional realist belief that language serves as 'a transparent medium that transmits a homologous picture of reality to the knowing mind,'[21] or whether one holds a social constructivist position that views the human subject as being trapped in a cultural and linguistic world of its own making, the primary distinction between language and reality remains in place. '[W]ords, concepts, ideas, and the like' may be perceived as 'accurately reflect[ing] or mirror[ing] the things to which they refer,' or they may be perceived as constituting a 'thick web of representations' that keeps the external world 'forever out of reach.'[22] Regardless of these distinctions, language continues to be thought of as being fundamentally separate from an external material reality.

For Barad, this fundamental division between human discursive practices and a supposedly separate material world is inherently flawed and untenable. Representationalism, Barad explains, is based on outdated metaphysical and scientific assumptions that display 'a deep mistrust of matter.'[23] Such assumptions either posit 'reality' as something that remains out of reach, or they elevate the human to the position of a God-like observer.[24] Either way, both of these positions generate inherently anthropocentric understandings of the world that prohibit human beings from truly engaging with anything other than themselves. Regardless of whether one thinks of language as representing some external nature or as being trapped in its own interiority,[25] such reflective paradigms are problematic because, in the final analysis, they merely serve to reflect the human back at itself. For Barad, social constructivist and traditional realist approaches to language are both equally caught in a reflective play of mirrors in which 'the epistemological gets bounced back and forth, but nothing more is seen.'[26] Representationalism traps human perception, knowledge and imagination in a specular engagement with the world in which it is the figure of the human that maintains primacy. Human beings see *themselves* in the world around them, or, at least, they continue to understand their so-called external reality through a distinctly anthropocentric lens, and this prohibits any further engagement with an 'outside' world, precisely because this would continue to be perceived *as* an outside.

In contrast to such representationalist understandings of the relationship between language and reality, Barad posits much more complex 'intra-active' entanglements between 'discursive practices' and 'material phenomena' in which language is not separate from this supposedly external world but a part of it.[27] For Barad, language does not *represent* the world like some metaphor or model but is instead intimately intertwined with and within it. Drawing on the work of Donna Haraway, Barad makes a distinction between the *reflective* and the *diffractive*, arguing that while reflective paradigms assume a relationship of correspondence but inherent separability between language and reality, diffractive modes of understanding recognise a different relationship (and a relationship *of* difference) with the so-called outside, in which the discursive and the material, matter and meaning, reality and knowledge are always already intimately implicated in and implied by one another.[28] Diffraction names '*a direct material engagement with the world*' and a recognition that 'meaning is not a property of individual words or groups of words but an ongoing performance of the world in its differential dance of intelligibility and unintelligibility.'[29] Human beings, meaning, language and any other form of so-called representation are not separate from an external reality but always co-constituted by it. As Barad puts it, 'matter and meaning are not separate elements'; matter *means* and meaning is *material*.[30]

Building on the work of Barad, a number of ecocritics and new materialist thinkers argue, therefore, that in addition to matter being vital and agen-tic,[31] 'active, self-creative, productive [and] unpredictable,'[32] it is also *textual*. Serenella Iovino and Serpil Oppermann posit that the world is comprised of 'storied matter' and that its 'material phenomena are knots in a vast net-work of agencies which can be "read" and interpreted as forming narratives, stories.' These 'stories,' we are told, are 'everywhere: in the air we breathe, the food we eat, in the things and beings of this world, within and beyond the human realm.'[33] '[M]atter and meaning,' these authors argue, 'constitute the fabric of our storied world,' and matter does not solely *appear* 'in texts' but *is* 'a text itself.'[34] A similar understanding of matter can be found in the work of Jeffrey Cohen, where this material textuality is explicitly linked to stone. Cohen argues that the propensity for matter to *mean* manifests itself most evidently in the materiality of the lithic, which he describes as being 'tangled in narrative,'[35] possessing its own 'numerous recording devices, repositories for nonlinguistic inscription, and indigenous but hard lithic poetics.'[36] Stone, Cohen explains, 'brings story into being'; it is 'a conveyance device that is at once linguistic, story-laden, thingly, and agentic.'[37] In its materiality, stone is *textual* because, like language, it allows for the transportation and production of meaning: it is 'a communication device that carries into distant futures the archive of a past otherwise lost,'[38] allowing human beings a glimpse into re-alities that may be spatially, temporally and materially inaccessible to them.

This description of lithic textuality echoes many of the images of inscrip-tion that appear in geological accounts of the earth's strata. But unlike in geology, where the notion of the earth as text appears to function primarily as a metaphor,[39] Cohen's description of stone as a 'communication device' is far more complex.[40] Here, the notion of lithic textuality is not presented as being merely metaphorical; for Cohen, there is *meaning in matter* and a *ma-teriality to meaning* that prevents these ideas from operating as simple analo-gies. Indeed, the very notion of metaphor is *itself* problematised by Cohen, who, borrowing a neologism by Lowell Duckert,[41] suggests that metaphor should perhaps be better thought of as 'matterphor'—as 'an ontological slid-ing, a tectonic veer, materiality coming into and out of figure.'[42] Metaphor is never merely representational because, like language more generally, it is always implicated in that which it supposedly represents.[43] And the notion of lithic textuality is also always more than some simple representationalist or reflective trope because the earth is itself involved in a textual movement that is akin to the transportation and conveyance of meaning in language.[44]

If the materiality of the earth is in itself in some sense metaphoric, as Cohen seems to suggest with his descriptions of stone as a 'material metaphor,' then linguistic 'metaphors' or 'matterphors' of a textual earth do not merely *represent* the earth as textual; they *recognise* it as being so. These aren't simple metaphors but a recognition of some inherent correspondence between the lithic and the textual.

Cohen's analysis of stone does not merely challenge preconceived assumptions about the nature of the lithic or of matter more generally; it also appears to disrupt traditional representationalist understandings of language and the anthropocentric assumptions they are based upon. Cohen's work shows how the lithic is 'irreducible to human use,' always 'exceed[ing] human framing,' but he also presents language itself as being equally 'inhuman,' arguing that 'narratives are always animated by multifarious vectors and heterogeneous possibilities not reducible to mere anthropomorphism.'[45] But at the same time, across his 'disanthropocentric' analysis of stone, one essential caveat always remains, a caveat that ultimately returns Cohen's notion of lithic textuality to the realm of human representation. 'The stories we know of stone *will always be human stories*,' Cohen argues, 'even if the cosmos they convey makes a problem of that category.'[46] As Cohen conceptualises them, these lithic stories might 'step out of anthropocentric frames,' but they can only really do so because they operate primarily from *within* them.[47] Cohen's work interrogates how the 'commonality' and 'breaching of ontological difference' between the human and non-human occurs and is given shape in human narrative,[48] but he does not seek to further interrogate how these 'material intimacies,' these 'strange likeness[es] and inalterable difference[s]' between human and stone and between the material and the textual, can be conceptualised outside of a direct human experience of them.[49] In the final analysis, Cohen's conceptualisation of lithic textuality thus remains tied to human ways of reading and engaging with the earth.

Iovino and Oppermann argue that within a materialist understanding of the world, 'language and reality, meanings and matter' must be thought 'together.'[50] Such an undertaking necessitates a reconceptualisation of matter, as can be seen in the many different manifestations of new materialist thought that have emerged over the past couple of decades.[51] But a rethinking of meaning and matter cannot occur without an accompanying reconceptualisation of textuality and language. It is here that certain aspects of new materialist thought can benefit from a more productive dialogue with deconstruction, as exemplified in the work of Vicki Kirby and Karen Barad.[52] In what follows, I draw on the work of these thinkers, as well as the broader insights that emerge from recent bio- and eco-deconstructive readings of

Derrida,[53] to explore the possibility of a language that is not simply bound to human systems of meaning, and of a non-human textuality that cannot simply be relegated to the realm of metaphor. Such a reconceptualisation of language and textuality is necessary, I argue, if we are to fundamentally reorient our thinking of matter and if we are to also radically reroute our reading of the Anthropocene. If the objective of this book is to go beyond the specular logic of the Anthropocene and find a way out of its self-reflexive gestures, then what is needed is a thinking of the lithic trace that does not remain tied to the possibility of a human reader, or even, more broadly, to human ways of understanding and 'reading' the world. Rather than assuming that the notion of lithic textuality functions as a rhetorical device that metonymically represents the ways in which human beings make sense of the world, we should seek to investigate how metaphor always functions as *more than* metaphor, and how language and textuality are never merely representational. Rather than assuming that the inscription of an anthropogenic 'signature' in the strata of the earth constitutes a *semiotic* trace *of* the human that exists *for* the human, we should seek to explore how this same trace also operates as a material inscription that is written and read in the myriad entanglements of material intra-actions by which it exists, persists and survives in the strata.

Derridean Textuality

Deconstruction has long been associated with questions of textuality, and much of Derrida's early work revolved around discussions of the trace and writing. Critics of Derrida often accuse him of myopically viewing the world through a radically constructivist framework in which reality is filtered through a lens of human textuality, allowing for no real exchange or interaction with the outside world.[54] But recently published texts such as the *Life Death* seminars first delivered by Derrida in 1975–1976,[55] and emerging bio- and eco-deconstructive readings of Derrida's work, paint a far more complex picture of the relationship Derrida envisages between language and material reality. As Fritsch, Lynes and Wood argue, the idea of a 'general textuality' that is mobilised by Derrida does not simply refer to human language but extends to many other human and non-human systems, behaviours and forms of existence.[56] 'Human language,' they explain, 'is only a particular system of marks or traces'; there are many other systems that share comparable structures of differential marks and generative patterns that far exceed human forms of language and semiotics.[57] The play of sameness and difference, repetition and deferral that Derrida identifies at the heart of human language is shared— always in differing ways—with other 'prelinguistic, nonanthropological marks or modes of existence,' and thus, in the work of Derrida, textuality should not be perceived as being limited to a specifically human system of writing.[58]

We can tease out the significance of these statements by considering Derrida's early discussions of writing at the beginning of *Of Grammatology*, where he notes that 'by a hardly perceptible necessity, it seems as though the concept of writing [. . .] is beginning to go beyond the extension of writing'; 'as if,' he tells us, 'what we call language could have been in its origin and in its end only a moment, an essential but determined mode, a phenomenon, an aspect, a species of writing.'[59] Derrida refers to the way that various non-linguistic activities are conceived of as forms of inscription—film, dance, the visual arts, music, sport, military-political engagements, cybernetics and, more importantly for our discussion here, biological and cellular processes. These activities and processes, Derrida notes, can all be considered forms of writing and textuality, whether this writing is 'literal or not and even if what it distributes in space is alien to the order of the voice.'[60] Christopher Johnson explains that what Derrida points to here is a growing tendency, in the decades leading up to the 1960s, for various phenomena—from the strictly anthropological to the more broadly biological—to be perceived in terms of linguistic and textual metaphors.[61] These 'epistemic shift[s]' within structuralism and poststructuralism colour Derrida's own understanding of textuality and inscription, informing the notion of a 'general writing' as developed in *Of Grammatology* and the works that followed.[62] But, importantly, as Johnson notes, the notion of a general writing or textuality that Derrida proposes and develops in his work—a general writing that extends to human systems and practices *as well as* non-human biological processes—'is not simply metaphor,' or, at least, it is not an 'idle' or 'innocent' metaphor; it is 'both metaphor and more than metaphor.'[63] Derrida is not merely concerned with the way that phenomena can be *represented* or *understood* as forms of inscription—he is concerned with the way that these phenomena actually *function as writing*. As Johnson explains, 'following the first movement of deconstruction, or rather implicit in its very movement, is the formulation of a general theory of "writing" as a fundamental structure of phenomena.'[64]

As several commentators have noted, Derrida's reference to genetics in *Of Grammatology* pre-empts his more thorough exploration of questions of biological textuality and inscription in the *Life Death* seminar.[65] Here Derrida explores the idea that genetic memory operates '*like* a language, with a code, a message, and a possible translation of messages.'[66] But in his reading of the work of the biologist François Jacob, the analogical or metaphorical relationship implied by this '*like*' is complexified and problematised. This is no simple metaphor or analogy because there is something *inherently* textual about the workings of genetic and cellular reproduction. Discussing Jacob's *The Logic of Life*,[67] Derrida argues that 'what could have appeared, more or less naively, to be the limited condition of philology, of literary criticism, of the science of documents and archives, etc., namely, having as its ultimate referent something that we used to call text and that we believed we understood under this name, this condition is now shared by genetics or the science of the living in general.'[68] The notion of biological textuality is no mere metaphor or analogy because genetic and cellular reproduction functions in a way that is 'fundamentally homogeneous' with the supposed model of textuality that is used to describe it.[69] There is 'a homogeneity (differentiated, but of the same type) between [the] productions of the living being called man (texts, in the narrow sense, computers, programs, and so on) and the functioning of genetic reproduction.'[70] Thus, as David Wills explains in his reading of this seminar, 'the concept of life itself cannot be defined or function outside of what Derrida calls "text,"' and 'what Derrida's seminar demonstrates with extraordinary clarity is that living cannot be a matter of reproduction without also being a matter of text, trace, and *différance*: text, trace, and *différance* are the facts of life.'[71]

But if the notion of analogy is problematised in Derrida's seminar, it is not merely because genetic reproduction is inherently textual—it is also because the very movement of *analogy* itself partakes in the same kinds of 'textual' processes under discussion. At the heart of the textual processes that Jacob identifies as taking place within the biological cell are the principles of *reproduction* and *selection* by which genetic material can replicate itself and evolve. But movements of reproduction and selection also underlie the structure of *metaphor*, in which an idea or an image is transported from one sphere of meaning to another and is recreated and reproduced through the maintaining and substituting of certain elements of difference and sameness.[72] And if reproduction and selection are foundational to both the biological processes being described *and* the metaphorical movements by which these descriptions take place, then what we have here is a complex intertwining of *different movements of difference* interacting with one another. If language and the genetic code both operate through the reproduction and selection of difference and sameness, and the 'analogical' or 'metaphorical' description of the relationship between these two systems is *itself* also structured by these same processes, then the relationship between these two systems and its manifestation in so-called metaphor are all different expressions of what Derrida refers to as *différance*—movements of difference and deferral that in language systems are what produce meaning.[73] This *différance* can be thought of as a general textuality that cuts across the biological processes of genetic reproduction that Jacob describes, the linguistic systems that he compares these biological processes to and the very structures of analogy and metaphor by which he recognises these relationships.[74] This textuality manifests itself in these different systems, always in differing and deferring ways, and the comparisons and analogies by which we try to make sense of this difference are themselves also direct but different manifestations of it.

In the way it is being used here, therefore, textuality should be understood neither merely *literally* (as referring solely to human language) nor simply *metaphorically* (as a straightforward linguistic representation of some non-linguistic other). Indeed, as Timothy Morton suggests in a discussion of Derridean textuality, 'the difference between what counts as a mere metaphor and what counts as non-metaphorical reality collapses when thinking engages text seriously.'[75] Textuality encompasses the movements of *différance* in language, but it also relates to other non-linguistic manifestations of *différance* in ways that are not merely metaphorical or analogical. The linguistic and non-linguistic phenomena being reflected upon here *all* partake in these movements and processes in different ways, and the relationships between them—encapsulated in the so-called metaphors that we use—themselves also take shape through the play of such differences. If we think the notion of text 'rigorously,' Morton explains, then we see that it is not some linguistic model that can simply be brought in to understand an external reality that remains non-textual and separate to it.[76] In the movement of its own meaning, textuality is implied in the processes that it is itself used to describe. In their very textuality and metaphoricity, textual 'metaphors' are differentially implicated in the phenomena they refer to. Using Barad's terminology, the Derridean notion of general textuality could thus be thought of as a *diffractive* (rather than reflective) paradigm, something that is both a 'metaphor' and 'more than a metaphor' and that 'not only brings the reality of entanglements to light' but 'is itself an entangled phenomenon.'[77]

Textuality Beyond Life

The Derridean notion of textuality offers us a way forward in our conceptualisation of the Anthropocene because it provides a way of thinking lithic marks of difference not as representational signs or signals that exist semiotically *for us* but as forms of material inscription that are engaged in their own movements of textuality. The persistence of certain lithic traces or 'inscriptions' in the strata of the earth is not bound to a human semiotic framework—although in the context of discourses on the Anthropocene it is often read as such. The continued existence of the lithic trace is *material*, and we must 'read' it in an equally materialist way if we are to rethink some of the most basic anthropocentric assumptions that underlie the notion of the Anthropocene. Such a 'reading' necessitates going beyond the limits and boundaries of what we generally think of as text (while also going beyond the limits and boundaries of what we think of as 'reading') in order to engage with the possibility of a textuality that structures the workings of matter. This material textuality can be *diffractively identified* by us as being textual, but it is not dependent on our recognition of it as such. It is a textuality that arises, always differently and differentially, out of the myriad intra-active configurations by which matter shapes and takes shape, and although we can develop a diffractive language with which to think its existence, it is not predicated on the presence or absence of such thought. Thinking such textuality can allow us to engage with forms of materiality that are not human or living (although they may in many ways be implicated in and intertwined with the discursive, material and biological practices of human beings and other living entities), and it can reorient our understanding of presence and absence in ways that transform how we grant value and significance to the material world.

My consideration of Derridean textuality in the discussions above focussed on the ways in which *biological* processes can be diffractively recognised (through metaphors that are not just metaphors) as constituting forms of textual inscription. But can this understanding of textuality be extended beyond the realm of the living? Could there be other movements of textuality and *différance* that cut across the boundaries of what Richard Iveson describes as 'the most traditional and pervasively normative of all metaphysical binaries'—that between life and non-living matter?[78] In her engagement with Derridean theory, Vicki Kirby identifies a certain textuality at work in a lightning storm and argues that electrical fields can also constitute 'expressions' or a 'conversation' that 'might be understood as instantiations of the graphematic (grammatological) structure' elaborated on by Derrida.[79] Meanwhile, Jeremy Butman notes that 'expression, as arche-writing, is not limited to the human, but traverses the borders of logic, speech, and even life,' including 'evolution and genetic inscription' but also 'fossilization [and] carbon decomposition.'[80] And Timothy Morton claims that what text 'includes, what it touches' consists of 'life forms' but also the 'Earth itself.'[81] Textuality, these authors suggest, does not merely manifest itself in the workings of language and life, it also diffractively extends *beyond* life to the nature of supposedly inert matter.

One of the key issues here relates to the question of reproduction. The self-reproducibility of organic structures is generally thought of as constituting one of the most fundamental principles of life, distinguishing living beings from inanimate matter.[82] And it is this principle that allows François Jacob to draw a parallel between genetic structures and written text. As Derrida notes in his reading of Jacob, 'what was discovered with the fourth-order structure [the discovery of DNA], and the model corresponding to this discovery, is the text, the fact that reproduction, an essential structure of the living, functions like a text.'[83] In Jacob's reading, the 'textuality' of genetic reproduction appears to constitute a fundamental attribute of the living, one that could not be shared with inanimate matter, precisely because such matter does not have the ability to reproduce. As Derrida explains it, 'reproduction is [. . .] defined as the very essence or the essential property of the living, what is proper to the living, livingness itself, its *ousia* and its *aitia*, its being-living, its essence-existence, the efficient and final cause, the final outcome of the efficient cause.'[84] Indeed, this positing of reproduction as the essence of life marks 'the essentiality of essence' because the idea of self-reproduction[85] reveals a supposed interiority, autonomy and self-sufficiency in the living organism or in the cell that is the essence of what essence should be: 'namely, to have one's principle of being in oneself and not in some accident coming from outside.'[86]

But it is this very notion of some textual 'essence' of the living that Derrida seeks to deconstruct through his reading. It is not quite *self-reproducibility*— the creation and recreation of the self-same—that constitutes biological textuality. This reproducibility must be mediated by difference and otherness for the production and creation of life to occur. This is most evident in sexual reproduction, where new life is created *out of* a breaking down of the boundaries between distinct genetic codes. But it is also evident in self-replicating bacteria that divide to create supposedly identical copies of themselves. Here supplementarity takes the shape of variations and mutations within the genetic code that allow for difference to be created out of the repetition of supposed sameness,[87] and it is evident in the swapping and switching of genes across different bacteria that renders any rigid distinction between asexual bacterial reproduction and the sexual activity of other types of organisms less straightforward.[88] It is as a result of such *differential* processes of reproduction (reiterations of difference *and* sameness) that new biological structures are brought to life, and this reproduction is also mediated by external processes of selection that determine which kinds of reiterations can survive and in turn reproduce within complex entangled systems of natural selection.

The reproduction of biological structures and organisms thus involves 'internal' mutations and variations as well as the influence of 'external' environmental factors. And the textuality of life does not simply exist or occur *within* the cell, as some attribute or essence of it—an expression of its innermost workings—but it arises out of the differential relationships and exchanges that constantly negotiate and renegotiate the limits of these boundaries. Derrida draws attention to the way that the textuality that Jacob recognises within the deepest recesses of the living cell cannot be said to function as some kind of internal *essence* of life—not because this textuality is *unnecessary* for life to take place but because it itself works through complex negotiations of internal and external differences that reveal how life is, *in its very own supposed essence*, constituted out of otherness. As Derrida notes, there is always 'a structural outside of the cell without which it would not reproduce itself and which thus makes of the *itself*, of the relation to self of re-production, an always fissured and open structure, a system that functions only insofar as it is in relation to the other or to the outside.'[89] The textuality that Derrida speaks of occurs at the points at which processes within the cell are mediated by difference and otherness, both *within* and *outside* of what we think of as being internal to the cell itself. Derrida explains that 'whenever one speaks of textuality, the value of relations of force, of a difference of force, an economics of agnostics, will be just as irreducible. Just like the opening to the outside of every textual system at the very moment it re-marks itself and re-inscribes itself.'[90] And, discussing the feedback loops that regulate every system, whether 'living or not,' he further emphasises that there is a 'structural opening' that 'makes untenable all the simple oppositions between inside and outside,' and that there is a 'supplementarity [. . .] inscribed in the very definition of every system, every living or non-living system.'[91]

The notion of textuality that emerges out of Derrida's deconstruction of Jacob's metaphors and analogies shows us how what appears to be most essential to life is precisely that which *cuts across* the parameters of the living, traversing the perceived insularity of the genetic code and the boundaries of the living cell and the organism. The textuality of life does not reside in the innermost workings of an organism, a cell or a genetic code and its ability to self-reproduce; the textuality of life consists of the constant inter- and intra-active mediation and negotiation of these structures and processes with that which supposedly exists outside of them. And it is here that we can locate the point at which the textuality inherent to the biological processes of life can be differently and diffractively recognised in the workings of supposedly inert matter. The exchange and circulation of energy, the production and reproduction of different formations of matter (although not necessarily its self-reproduction), the creation and recreation of different forces and different systems in and across boundaries—in a word, the *movements* of differential intra-activity that underwrite the processes of biological life—are not particular or peculiar to living beings but are how large extended networks of different forms of living *and* non-living matter exist and persist upon the earth. If we lift our gaze up from the individual organism or isolated object, away from the boundaries, outlines and perimeters by which we define and conceptualise individuated entities (whether living or not), and we instead view living and non-living entities through the intricate material processes and exchanges that constitute them, then we can begin to see how the notion of textuality that I am outlining here can cut across different forms of animate and inanimate matter and traverse the conceptual boundary we have put in place between life and non-life.

Material and Discursive Intra-Activity

It is useful here to bring the Derridean notion of textuality into dialogue with Barad's understanding of matter as '*substance in its intra-active becoming—not a thing, but a doing, a congealing of agency.*' Matter, Barad explains, whether living or not, should not be thought of as a preformed entity or identity that exists and acts; it should instead be viewed in terms of the processes and intra-actions that allow for such existence to take place. Matter, Barad explains, '*is a stabilizing and destabilizing process of interactive intra-activity*'; it refers '*to the materiality and materialization of phenomena,* not to an assumed, inherent, fixed property of abstract, independently existing objects.'[92] The notion of Derridean textuality that I am developing here closely relates to this concept of intra-activity whereby entities are constituted by the differential relations and processes that occur within and outside of themselves in ways that problematise the very distinction between an inside and an outside. Textuality does not *belong* to the living or to life like some internal process or structure. Indeed, as Derrida notes, 'there is no such thing as *the* living and *the* text.'[93] And, therefore, this idea cannot simply be used to define and characterise life in distinction to non-living matter. The movements and processes of differentiation being considered here are what *cut across* different kinds of matter and the distinctions we bring to bear upon them, always in different, differential and diffractive ways. An understanding of this textuality does not flatten the distinction between different kinds of matter, or posit an undifferentiated homogeneity in which everything appears the same.[94] But it does problematise and challenge any attempt to reduce these complex, multiple and intra-active relationships of difference and sameness to a single opposition or distinction based on some idea of an essence of life and the living.

Such a notion of textuality thus allows us to see how different forms of matter, whether living or not, inter- and intra-act with and within each other in ways that always implicate them in that which they supposedly are not. This intra-action, described by Barad as 'the mutual constitution of entangled agencies,'[95] problematises any simple notion of identity, and it fundamentally undermines any simple conception of presence. If different forms of matter are always constituted through difference and otherness, always formed out of their intra-actions with that which is outside of them, then they can never be said to be fully present. It is here that we can return to the idea of spectrality discussed in previous chapters. I argued earlier that a thorough re-evaluation of the notion of the Anthropocene would benefit from a *hauntological* reading of the anthropocenic trace that would not be predicated on the relative presence or absence of the human. The material understanding of spectrality that underlies my reading of the Anthropocene does not take as its starting point some ghostly figure of the human that would remain present in its absence or absent in its continued presence, and it is not predicated on the existence of some spectral anthropogenic trace or lingering anthropomorphic gaze that would continue to confirm the significance and value of the human. Instead, the spectrality I am concerned with is one that recognises how any so-called *presence* (whether material, biological or human) is composed out of complex intra-active relationships that cut across the boundaries of the self, the organism or the object, problematising any simple notion of autonomy or individuality and destabilising the conceptual frameworks by which we distinguish between the human, other forms of life and other forms of matter.

Rather than repeat the anthropocentric and specular gestures of the Anthropocene in which the lithic trace appears as a sign *of* and *for* the human— a sign that asserts the continued presence of the human even in its supposed absence—the notion of textuality I am developing here allows for a *different* and *differential* conceptualisation of the lithic trace that is not predicated on such notions of presence. The anthropogenic marks of difference left behind in the earth's strata can be recognised as constituting textual 'inscriptions' not because they can be *read as signs* within a human semiotic framework but because they arise out of complex material relations of intra-activity (both human *and* non-human, living *and* non-living) that share differential and diffractive relationships with the play of *différance* that we can recognise in human language. This is a textuality that extends beyond the human and its 'metaphorical' conceptions of the world, but it is a textuality that is itself also diffractively implicated in these metaphors, allowing us a means with which to engage with that which we think of as existing 'outside' of us while also deconstructing the very notion of an outside, showing us that we are always implicated in that which we distinguish ourselves from.

It is in this sense that the notion of lithic textuality can function as a diffractive paradigm for thinking the Anthropocene. This paradigm does not merely *refer* to the differential movements of intra-activity that underlie the workings of different kinds of matter; in its very metaphoricity, the notion of lithic textuality itself *enacts* these differential movements, inviting us to reconceptualise the relationship between human language and non-human matter in a way that can allow us to reassess the value and significance we grant to each. Such diffractive paradigms do not merely draw our attention to the complex relationships of difference out of which different forms of matter emerge; they are themselves conceptually constituted *out of* such movements of difference, and, as human discursive practices, they also have the potential to *enact* and *effect* difference by influencing the way we perceive, understand and behave in the world. In what follows, I explore the possibility of other different but related supplementary paradigms that can allow us to reorient our thinking of the Anthropocene in ways that do not exceptionalise the human or posit its continued value and significance upon the earth but that instead invite us to find better means of *living* and *surviving*, beyond, perhaps, the ways in which we have so far understood either of these terms.

Notes

1. See, for instance, Simon L. Lewis and Mark A. Maslin, "Defining the Anthropocene," *Nature* 519, no. 7542 (March 2015): 171, https://doi.org/10.1038/nature14258; Colin N. Waters et al., "The Anthropocene Is Functionally and Stratigraphically Distinct from the Holocene," *Science* 351, no. 6269 (January 2016): 137–47, https://doi.org/10.1126/science.aad2622; and Jan Zalasiewicz et al., "Are We Now Living in the Anthropocene?" *GSA Today* 18, no. 2 (February 2008): 4, https://doi.org/10.1130/GSAT01802A.1.

2. Commenting on notions of textual inscription in present-day discussions of the Anthropocene, Bronislaw Szerszynski recalls the geologist David Thomas Ansted's (1814–1880) metaphor of 'the great stone book of nature' and his description of geology as the practice of reading this earthly text (Bronislaw Szerszynski, "The End of the End of Nature: The Anthropocene and the Fate of the Human," *The Oxford Literary Review* 34, no. 2 (December 2012): 169, https://doi.org/10.3366/olr.2012.0040). Similarly, Benjamin Morgan refers to the work of the Victorian geologist John Phillips (1800–1874), who described geological time as being written into the earth's rocks (Benjamin Morgan, "Scale as Form: Thomas Hardy's Rocks and Stars," in *Anthropocene Reading: Literary History in Geologic Times*, ed. Tobias Menely and Jesse Oak Taylor (University Park: Pennsylvania State University Press, 2017), 134). One can add to this genealogy the geologist Adam Sedgwick (1785–1873), for whom the earth constituted a 'volume' of natural history (Adam Sedgwick, "Presidential Ad-

dress to the Geological Society," *The Philosophical Magazine and Annals of Philosophy* 7, no. 39 (1830): 308); and Charles Lyell (1797–1875), whose own conceptualisations of the earth as a written book prompted Charles Darwin to refer to the earth's crust 'as a history of the world imperfectly kept, and written in a changing dialect' (Charles Darwin, *The Origin of Species* (London: Penguin, 1968), 316).

3. Discussing the semiotic nature of geology, Victor R. Baker argues that while it may not be 'a method for doing geology, semiotics provides a means of describing the highly productive reasoning processes of geologists' (Victor R. Baker, "Geosemiosis," *Geological Society of America Bulletin* 111, no. 5 (May 1999): 633, https://doi .org/10.1130/0016-7606(1999)111<0633:G>2.3.CO;2).

4. Jan Zalasiewicz, *The Earth After Us: What Legacy Will Humans Leave in the Rocks?* (Oxford: Oxford University Press, 2008), 15, 6.

5. Tobias Menely and Jesse Oak Taylor, eds., *Anthropocene Reading: Literary History in Geologic Times* (University Park: Pennsylvania State University Press, 2017), 6–7. As is standard practice in geology, for the Anthropocene to be declared an official geological time unit particular geochemical markers must be identified and they must themselves be marked out by what is commonly referred to as a 'Golden Spike'—an actual metal peg or plaque that is drilled into the rock to indicate where in the strata a particular geological time unit begins. As a human-fashioned marker used to signal the position of anthropogenic geochemical markers, the Anthropocene golden spike functions as a sign of a sign, drawing attention to the fundamentally semiotic nature of these practices.

6. "Results of Binding Vote by AWG," Anthropocene Working Group, May 21, 2019, http://quaternary.stratigraphy.org/working-groups/anthropocene/.

7. Tobias Boes and Kate Marshall, "Writing the Anthropocene: An Introduction," *Minnesota Review*, no. 83 (November 2014): 64; emphasis added.

8. Menely and Taylor, *Anthropocene Reading*, 3.

9. Zalasiewicz, *Earth After Us*, 120, 138, 118, 144.

10. Szerszynski, "The End of the End of Nature," 165, 180.

11. Boes and Marshall, "Writing the Anthropocene," 63.

12. Zalasiewicz, *Earth After Us*, 17.

13. Morgan, "Scale as Form," 137–38.

14. Jeffrey Jerome Cohen and Lowell Duckert, eds., *Elemental Ecocriticism: Thinking with Earth, Air, Water, and Fire* (Minneapolis: University of Minnesota Press, 2015), 9.

15. Serenella Iovino and Serpil Oppermann, *Material Ecocriticism* (Bloomington: Indiana University Press, 2014), 6–7.

16. Claire Colebrook, *Death of the PostHuman: Essays on Extinction*, Vol. 1 (Ann Arbor, MI: Open Humanities Press, 2015), 23.

17. Even when commentators invite their readers to imagine non-human forms of intelligent life discovering and reading the remnants of our anthropocenic world, these beings remain distinctly anthropomorphic. The creatures that Jan Zalasiewicz envisions discovering signs of human civilisation in the strata of the earth, for

instance, sport non-human 'tails and sharp claws' (Zalasiewicz, *Earth After Us*, xii), but they are undoubtedly anthropomorphic in their scientific curiosity and their desire to record and narrate their journey of discovery upon this earth.

18. Szerszynski, "The End of the End of Nature," 167.

19. Karen Barad, *Meeting the Universe Halfway: Quantum Physics and the Entanglement of Matter and Meaning* (Durham, NC: Duke University Press, 2007), 133, 323.

20. Barad, *Meeting the Universe Halfway*, 46.

21. Barad, *Meeting the Universe Halfway*, 97.

22. Barad, *Meeting the Universe Halfway*, 86, 137.

23. Barad, *Meeting the Universe Halfway*, 133.

24. Barad, *Meeting the Universe Halfway*, 137, 233.

25. Barad, *Meeting the Universe Halfway*, 86.

26. Barad, *Meeting the Universe Halfway*, 135.

27. Barad, *Meeting the Universe Halfway*, 44.

28. Barad, *Meeting the Universe Halfway*, 81.

29. Barad, *Meeting the Universe Halfway*, 49, 149.

30. Barad, *Meeting the Universe Halfway*, 3.

31. Jane Bennett, *Vibrant Matter: A Political Ecology of Things* (Durham, NC: Duke University Press, 2010).

32. Diana Coole and Samantha Frost, eds., *New Materialisms: Ontology, Agency, and Politics* (Durham, NC: Duke University Press, 2010), 9.

33. Iovino and Oppermann, *Material Ecocriticism*, 1.

34. Iovino and Oppermann, *Material Ecocriticism*, 5–6.

35. Jeffrey Jerome Cohen, *Stone: An Ecology of the Inhuman* (Minneapolis: University of Minnesota Press, 2016), 12.

36. Cohen, *Stone*, 35.

37. Cohen, *Stone*, 4.

38. Cohen, *Stone*, 11.

39. Such an understanding of the notion of the lithic trace is indicative of the way that metaphor is often perceived in scientific writing more broadly. Metaphor is deemed to be a heuristic tool or a rhetorical flourish that reflects and represents an outside reality, but one that has no real bearing on the material world. Explaining the distinction between 'good' and 'bad' metaphors in scientific writing, the palaeontologist, evolutionary biologist and science historian Stephen Jay Gould argues that no one metaphor can ever be 'truer to nature' than another, 'for neither [. . .] lies "out there" in the woods' (Stephen J. Gould, "Glow, Big Glowworm," *Natural History* 95, no. 12 (1986): 16). For Gould, metaphor is distinct and separate from the world; it is a rhetorical device that translates an outside reality into an image that can be understood by the human mind, but there is no further connection between this image and the actual reality that it represents. One set of metaphors may be said to be 'better' than another because they serve a superior heuristic purpose, but they nevertheless remain mere 'spectacles of our mind' (Gould, "Glow," 16).

40. Cohen, *Stone*, 11.

41. See Cohen and Duckert, *Elemental Ecocriticism*, 11.

42. Cohen, *Stone*, 4–5.

43. As Barad herself notes, 'matter and meaning, the literal and the figurative, are never as separate as we like to pretend' (Barad, *Meeting the Universe Halfway*, 362).

44. Cohen, *Stone*, 4–5.

45. Cohen, *Stone*, 54, 4, 36.

46. Cohen, *Stone*, 9; emphasis added.

47. Cohen, *Stone*, 33–34.

48. Cohen, *Stone*, 54.

49. Cohen, *Stone*, 9, 54.

50. Iovino and Oppermann, *Material Ecocriticism*, 4.

51. As Iovino and Oppermann note, across its different manifestations, new materialism dismantles the idea that matter is 'passive, inert, unable to convey any independent expression of meaning' (Iovino and Oppermann, *Material Ecocriticism*, 2). For various discussions of this, see Stacy Alaimo and Susan Heckman, eds., *Material Feminisms* (Bloomington: Indiana University Press, 2008); Coole and Frost, *New Materialisms*; and Rick Dolphijn and Iris van der Tuin, *New Materialism: Interviews and Cartographies* (Ann Arbor, MI: Open Humanities Press, 2012).

52. The work of Karen Barad and Vicki Kirby is described by Gambel, Hanan and Nail as constituting a form of 'performative new materialism' in which 'ontology and epistemology are inherently co-implicated and mutually constituting' in a way that 'neither requires nor is in any sense restricted to humans' (Christopher N. Gamble, Joshua S. Hanan, and Thomas Nail, "What Is New Materialism?" *Angelaki* 24, no. 6 (December 2019): 111–34, https://doi.org/10.1080/0969725X.2019.1684704122.

53. See, for instance: Dawne McCance, *The Reproduction of Life Death: Derrida's La vie la mort* (New York: Fordham University Press, 2019); Francesco Vitale, *Biodeconstruction: Jacques Derrida and the Life Sciences*, trans. Mauro Senatore (Albany, NY: SUNY Press, 2018); the double issue "Of Biodeconstruction," ed. Erin Obodiac, *Postmodern Culture* 28, no. 3 (May 2018) and 29, no. 1 (September 2018); Philippe Lynes, *Futures of Life Death on Earth: Derrida's General Ecology* (London: Rowman & Littlefield International, 2018); Matthias Fritsch, Philippe Lynes, and David Wood, eds., *Eco-Deconstruction: Derrida and Environmental Philosophy* (New York: Fordham University Press, 2018); and Mauro Senatore, *Germs of Death: The Problem of Genesis in Jacques Derrida* (Albany, NY: SUNY Press, 2018).

54. See Jonathan Basile, "Misreading Generalised Writing: From Foucault to Speculative Realism and New Materialism," *Oxford Literary Review* 40, no. 1 (July 2018): 20–37, https://doi.org/10.3366/olr.2018.0236.

55. Jacques Derrida, *Life Death*, trans. Pascale-Anne Brault and Michael Naas (Chicago: University of Chicago Press, 2020).

56. Fritsch, Lynes, and Wood, *Eco-Deconstruction*, 7.

57. Fritsch, Lynes, and Wood, *Eco-Deconstruction*, 8.

58. Fritsch, Lynes, and Wood, *Eco-Deconstruction*, 8.

59. Jacques Derrida, *Of Grammatology*, trans. Gayatri Chakravorty Spivak (corrected ed.) (Baltimore: Johns Hopkins University Press, 1998), 6–8.

60. Derrida, *Grammatology*, 9.

61. Christopher Johnson, *System and Writing in the Philosophy of Jacques Derrida* (Cambridge: Cambridge University Press, 1993), 1–4.

62. Johnson, *System and Writing*, 4.

63. Derrida, *Grammatology*, 172–73, 190.

64. Johnson, *System and Writing*, 8.

65. See, for instance, Vitale, *Biodeconstruction*, 2, and McCance, *Reproduction of Life Death*, 27. David Wills notes that Derrida's ongoing interest in the life sciences, from his early texts and seminars to his final seminar on *The Beast and the Sovereign*, 'might be seen to develop what Derrida delineates in the 1971 essay "White Mythology" as an 'epistemological ambivalence of metaphor, which always provokes, retards, *follows* the movement of the concept, [and] perhaps finds its chosen field in the life sciences' (David Wills, *Inanimation: Theories of Inorganic Life* (Minneapolis: University of Minnesota Press, 2016), 8).

66. Derrida, *Life Death*, 15. For discussions of how textual and linguistic metaphors have been used to describe the human genome and DNA more generally, see Lily E. Kay, *Who Wrote the Book of Life?: A History of the Genetic Code* (Stanford, CA: Stanford University Press, 2000); and Judith Roof, *The Poetics of DNA* (Minneapolis: University of Minnesota Press, 2007).

67. Derrida translates Jacob's title as 'The Logic of the Living' (see Derrida, *Life Death*, 3, trans. note 4).

68. Derrida, *Life Death*, 78.

69. Derrida, *Life Death*, 81.

70. Derrida, *Life Death*, 90.

71. Wills, *Inanimation*, 12–13.

72. See Derrida, *Life Death*, 58–59, 132.

73. See "Différance" for Derrida's reading of Saussure (Jacques Derrida, "Différance," in *Margins of Philosophy*, trans. Alan Bass (Brighton: Harvester Press, 1982)). As Timothy Morton puts it, 'Saussure gave a precise environmental definition of the linguistic sign. [. . .] Signs are interdependent. The existence of a sign implies coexistence with other signs' (Timothy Morton, "Ecology as Text, Text as Ecology," *The Oxford Literary Review* 32, no. 1 (July 2010): 1–17, https://doi.org/10.3366/E0305149810000G112).

74. In her discussion of Derrida's seminar, Dawne McCance explains that it is 'différence [. . .] that characterizes the two DNA strands that come together during sexual reproduction' and that also structures 'molecular transferences and translations between DNA and RNA' (McCance, *Reproduction of Life Death*, 31). Meanwhile, Francesco Vitale argues that 'between the genetic and the symbolic, between nature and culture, there is neither identity not opposition but *différance*' (Francesco Vitale, "Reading the Programme: Jacques Derrida's Deconstruction of Biology," *Postmodern Culture* 28, no. 3 (May 2018) [n.p.], and Erin Obodiac notes that 'between cerebral

and genetic memory, instead of analogy, there is a differential relation: différance and the mnemo-technics of the trace subtend the cerebral and the genetic' (Erin Obodiac, "Introduction: Of Biodeconstruction (Part I)," n.p.).

75. Morton, "Ecology as Text," 2–3.

76. Morton, "Ecology as Text," 3.

77. Barad, *Meeting the Universe Halfway*, 71–73.

78. Richard Iveson, "Being Without Life: On the Trace of Organic Chauvinism with Derrida and DeLanda," in *Philosophy After Nature*, ed. Rosi Braidotti and Rick Dolphijn (London: Rowman & Littlefield International, 2017), 186.

79. Vicki Kirby, *Quantum Anthropologies: Life at Large* (Durham, NC: Duke University Press, 2011), 12.

80. Jeremy Butman, "Deconstructive Empiricism: Science and Metaphor in Derrida's Early Work," *Derrida Today* 12, no. 2 (November 2019): 122, https://doi.org/10.3366/drt.2019.0205.

81. Morton, "Ecology as Text," 2.

82. The distinction between animate life and inanimate matter is foundational to modern biology and is based on the idea that reproduction constitutes some kind of essence of life. As David Wills notes in his discussion of François Jacob's *The Logic of Life*, from the beginning of the 19th century, 'life' has been conceived of as a 'positive principle' distinguishable from its negative counterpart: 'on the one side, there [is] inorganic, non-living, inanimate, inert matter, on the other an organic that breeds, feeds, and reproduces' (Wills, *Inanimation*, 3).

83. Derrida, *Life Death*, 79–80.

84. Derrida, *Life Death*, 86.

85. This is, Derrida tells us, what Jacob means when he speaks of reproduction. Derrida notes that 'Jacob always says re-production whenever he is clearly describing self-reproduction,' but 'there are non-living things that re-produce without re-producing themselves,' and therefore it is 'this bending back upon the self, this auto-affection' that 'is an essential fold of the structure' (Derrida, *Life Death*, 83).

86. Derrida, *Life Death*, 87.

87. See Derrida, *Life Death*, 93–94.

88. This is generally referred to as horizontal gene transfer and is discussed by Derrida in *Life Death* (112–13). Merlin Sheldrake explains this principle by drawing an analogy with the exchange of information with a cultural milieu: 'One bacterium could acquire a trait from another bacterium "horizontally." Characteristics acquired horizontally are those that aren't inherited "vertically" from one's parents. One picks them up along the way. We're used to the principle. When we learn or teach something, we're part of a horizontal exchange of information. Much of human culture and behaviour is transmitted in this fashion' (Merlin Sheldrake, *Entangled Life: How Fungi Make Our Worlds, Change Our Minds, and Shape Our Futures* (London: The Bodley Head, 2020), 87). Sheldrake's comparison is significant because it draws attention to the differential relationship between life and text that I am discussing here.

89. Derrida, *Life Death*, 132.

90. Derrida, *Life Death*, 124.

91. Derrida, *Life Death*, 126–27.

92. Barad, *Meeting the Universe Halfway*, 210.

93. Derrida, *Life Death*, 120.

94. One possible objection to the argument being outlined here is that the notion of general textuality flattens the distinction between the human and the non-human and glosses over the very real differences that exist between them, levelling out reality into one undifferentiated plane of textuality and discursivity. According to such an objection, the concept of general textuality would present everything in anthropomorphic terms—it would constitute a projection of human agency, language, intentionality and intelligence onto an external nature, ignoring the very real differences that exist between human systems of language, biological and material processes. Where such an objection falters is in its characterisation of this shared textuality as being based on a principle of *sameness*. Reflecting on her own interpretation of Derrida's general textuality as a 'global articulation *of and by* the world,' Vicki Kirby argues that the real challenge is to understand that what is being conceptualised here is not a simple relationship of identity but one that destabilises the very notions of sameness and difference as they are commonly understood (Kirby, *Quantum Anthropologies*, 34, 71, 92). Although these textualities 'can be read as different expressions of the same phenomenon' (Kirby, *Quantum Anthropologies*, viii), this does not mean that there are no differences between them. Textuality, as Derrida shows us in his work, is differential; it is the reiterative and deferred play of difference and sameness that constitutes language. It is not the *same* differentiality that is inscribed in different living and material processes. A general textuality does not consist of different systems of differences being shown to be *analogous* to one another; it instead requires that we think the relationships between these different systems of difference *differently* and *differentially*.

95. Barad, *Meeting the Universe Halfway*, 33.

CHAPTER THREE

~

Entangled Survivance

Material Inscriptions of Otherness

The Derridean notion of textuality, as I am developing it here, draws attention to the complex entanglements of intra-activity out of which different
material and discursive phenomena (both living and non-living, human and
non-human) are composed. As a diffractive paradigm that always functions
as more than some mere representational trope, the notion of textuality does
not merely *refer* to the way that the intra-activity of matter operates; it itself
also *enacts* forms of intra-active exchange that cut across different linguistic
realms to create meaning. Significantly, this intra-active performativity is
not simply *contained* within language; it can also traverse the always porous
boundaries between language and material reality, changing how human
beings view and interact with the world. Returning to the discussion of
metaphor introduced in the previous chapter, one could say here that textual
metaphors are always *more than* mere metaphors not just because they *enact*
what they are supposed to simply represent but because this enactment can
itself potentially also *act on* so-called outside reality by influencing the way
that human beings think and behave. The language with which we think
intra-activity *itself* also has the power to intra-actively intervene in the
world. To quote Karen Barad, these are 'patterns of difference that make
a difference.'[1] By tracking the different permutations of this intra-active
textuality—understood both as a discursive paradigm and as the material
intra-activity that such a paradigm diffractively 'refers' to—we can begin to
transform our understanding of the Anthropocene and rethink our relationships with different living and non-living entities.

A reconceptualisation of the notion of textuality, as well as a re-examination of how metaphor functions in relation to it, opens up the space for a diffractive reading of other ideas and paradigms that are central to our understanding of the Anthropocene. My exploration of lithic textuality in Chapter 2 invited an examination of the concept of *life* and its presumed distinction from that which is not living. Here I turn my attention to the way that the related notion of *survival*, or, to use the term favoured by Derrida, *survivance*, can also be thought of in terms of inanimate matter. As it is conceptualised through my reading of Derrida, this term highlights how complex processes of textuality (such as those discussed in Chapter 2) are constituted out of forms of exchange that are not limited to living beings but that cut across different kinds of life and matter. My exploration of this material survivance and textuality[2] lays the groundwork for a 'rereading' of the anthropocenic trace in Chapter 4 that does not rely on a semiotic understanding of the so-called signatures or signs in the earth's strata but considers how the traces of radioactivity embedded in the rock—these so-called signatures of the Anthropocene—will continue to exist, persist and survive *materially* for many millennia to come. As I show in what follows, tracking the movements of this survivance is crucial because it can allow us to break down the strict opposition between the living and the non-living, the animate and the inanimate to which different forms of matter have been reduced, and it can allow us to reassess the relative significance and value that we attribute to the different material realities we form part of.

Life, Text and Survivance

The previous chapter explored the relationship between 'life' and 'text' by considering how the Derridean notion of textuality can serve as more than a simple metaphor for the workings of biological life. In *Life Death*, Derrida deconstructs the biologist François Jacob's use of linguistic and textual metaphors in his explanations of DNA and cellular reproduction, allowing us to see how such metaphors always function as more than some mere representational trope because they are themselves intimately implicated in the movements of difference and deferral that they supposedly refer to. But in other works, Derrida also analyses how this same diffractive paradigm can operate in *reverse*: how the notion of *life* might itself also function as a metaphor, and, importantly, *more than* a metaphor, for texts and textuality. An exploration of this reversal can further reveal the diffractive nature of the relationship between the living and the textual, and, more importantly, it can open up the space for a thinking of 'life' and 'textuality' that is not limited to the strictly biological or linguistic but that pertains to the existence and persistence of non-living matter. As we shall see later on, such material textuality is exemplified in the traces of radioactive materials that can be said to 'live' and 'live on' in the earth's strata, existing and surviving in movements of difference and otherness that are both *conceptually comparable* to and *materially entangled* in the workings of biological life and human discursive practices.

In "Des Tour de Babel," Derrida considers the use of 'genealogical motifs and allusions—more or less than metaphorical' in Walter Benjamin's essay "The Task of the Translator."[3] Derrida comments on the way that Benjamin uses what 'could resemble a vitalist or geneticist metaphor' in speaking of texts as if they were alive.[4] But, Derrida notes, Benjamin's language is neither truly vitalist nor metaphoric because it operates within the space of a differential relationship between text and life that exceeds the metaphoric and also potentially destabilises any straightforward understanding of the concept of life.[5] Between what could be interpreted as a vitalist metaphor in Benjamin's text and the textual metaphors used by an author like François Jacob, there is a conceptual inversion that draws attention to what Derrida describes as the 'metaphoric catastrophe' by which life is entangled in textuality and textuality is entangled in life.[6] As Christopher Johnson explains it, this 'catastrophe' is that of the 'more than metaphor' by which 'not only is the term a germ, but the germ is, in the most general sense, a term.'[7] This 'catastrophe' is enacted in Derrida's notion of general textuality—a concept that functions, as we have seen, not simply as a metaphor but as a diffractive paradigm that is always implicated in that which it supposedly represents. But it can also manifest itself *differently*, in other paradigms that also draw attention to the structures of differentiality that underlie the living and the textual, revealing the space between these two concepts, and between the movements of *différance* that they refer to, to be *itself* differential and diffractive.

The notion of *survivance*, as it is conceptualised by Derrida and as I continue to develop it here, is one such paradigm. Within the context of Derrida's reading of Benjamin, the diffractive life of a text and the textuality of life are linked to the use of this one particular term. Discussing the possibility of a text *living* and *living on* as a result of its translation, Derrida isolates Benjamin's use of the German term 'Überleben,' translated into the French as '*survie*.'[8] This term, which appears as 'sur-vival' in the English translation of Derrida's text,[9] signifies both 'survival' and 'afterlife,'[10] thus drawing attention to the spectral implications of Benjamin's analysis. As Derrida explains it, Benjamin 'calls us to think life, starting from spirit or history and not from "organic corporeality" alone. There is life at the moment when "sur-vival" (spirit, history, works) exceeds biological life and death.'[11] The spectrality that haunts Benjamin's use of this term is not merely linked to the idea of a life that lives on after death—a translated text, for instance, that follows on from its predecessor and that could thus be thought of as a ghostly trace that keeps the original alive. 'Life' is spectral in Benjamin's essay because it is related to the concept of *non-biological life*—it traverses the boundaries between that which is biologically *alive* and something else, in a way that is not merely metaphorical. To quote David Wills's reading of Benjamin's essay, texts always '*live on otherwise*';[12] they always live *spectrally*, in some *other way*, outside of the opposition of life and death, beyond their own textual parameters and beyond the parameters of what is usually understood by the term 'life' itself.[13]

This spectrality is gestured towards in the use of the term 'sur-vival,' where the hyphen, introduced by the translator of Derrida's text, is intended to suggest 'the subliminal sense of more life and more than life'[14]—something that *exceeds* life without itself being alive in a biological sense. As Derrida suggests elsewhere, this 'more' should not be understood in terms of a superlative form of life but as something *other to life* (as well as an *otherness in life*[15]) that survives nevertheless. In *The Beast and the Sovereign II*, Derrida uses the term 'survivance' to describe 'a sense of survival that is neither life nor death pure and simple, a sense that is not thinkable on the basis of the opposition between life and death.' Despite 'the apparent grammar of the formation of the word (überleben or *forteleben*, living on or to survive, survival),' Derrida notes that this 'survival' is not '*above* life, like something sovereign (*superanus*) can be above everything.' It is a 'survival that is not more alive, nor indeed less alive, than life, or more or less dead than death, a sur-vivance that lends itself to neither comparative nor superlative.' Survivance 'is something other than life death, but a groundless ground from which are detached, identified, and opposed what we think we can identify under the name of death or dying (*Tod*, *Sterben*), like death properly so-called as opposed to some life properly so-called. It [Ça] begins with survival.'[16] Survivance does not point to something that simply lives or lives on within life or death; it is instead something *other* to life that is nevertheless implied *within* it, and something that is active *within* it while also remaining, persisting and surviving *outside* of it.

Derrida's description of survivance in *The Beast and the Sovereign II* occurs in the context of a discussion of how the book—any book, but in this particular case Daniel Defoe's *Robinson Crusoe*—*lives* and *survives* in a way that is other to the concept and the functioning of biological life while remaining in some way related to it. But Derrida also links the idea of survivance to the more general notion of the trace, noting that the book lives on 'like every trace [. . .] from its first moment on.'[17] This suggests the possibility of a broader understanding of survivance, one that is not limited to *actual* textual entities (such as *Robinson Crusoe* or the original and translated texts that Benjamin talks about in his essay) but that relates to the implicit textuality of *other* forms of material reality. An essay by Derrida composed of a series of diary fragments written between 1988 and 1989 and collected under the title "Biodegradables"[18] provides the material for such a reading, allowing for an exploration of the way that the 'life' of a text and the 'textuality' of life might both be diffractively related to other forms of *material survivance* that are neither biologically alive nor linguistically textual but that are engaged in differential movements and processes of inter- and intra-activity that can be recognised as implicitly 'textual' or spectrally 'alive' in other ways. It is within the diffractive space of these relationships between life, text and survivance—terms that cannot, we must remember, simply be reduced to mere metaphors or conceptual analogies—that we can begin to think the material textuality and spectral 'life' of something like a radioactive isotope inscribed into the strata of the earth.

The Biodegradability of Text

In "Biodegradables," Derrida engages in a series of detailed reflections on the possible life, death and survival of textual entities through a consideration of the notion of 'biodegradability.' The initial question that motivates Derrida's reflections in this essay is whether 'everything that is attached to words, everything that delivers itself over to words, everything that is delivered up by words' can be said to be biodegradable.[19] Derrida asks: 'Can one transpose onto "culture" the vocabulary of "natural waste treatment"—recycling, ecosystems, and so on [. . .]'; 'can one say that, given this or that condition, one publication is more biodegradable, more quickly decomposed than another';[20] are rhetoric and discourse not themselves 'in a constant state of recycling [. . . of] composition, decomposition, recomposition'; and can one 'speak nonfiguratively of biodegradability with regard to the identity attributed to a supposedly proper meaning.'?[21] What Derrida is essentially asking here is the same question that motivates Benjamin's reflections on literary works and their translations in "The Task of the Translator": Can a text be said to *survive*, and thus also *biodegrade*,[22] in a non-metaphorical sense? In his mixing of biological and linguistic registers, Derrida provides a preliminary response to this: he refers to 'the "bacteria" of language,' to 'hermeneutic microorganisms' living outside and within a text and to the '"ecosystem" of an archive.'[23] Life and text, Derrida suggests, are intimately implicated in one another because living organisms and textual entities are all engaged in processes of survivance—differential and diffractive operations of production and reproduction, decay and decomposition, recomposition and recycling that always extend beyond life and the living.

The relationship between biodegradability and survivance is made clear by Derrida as he discusses the way that the 'life' of a text is simultaneously also its 'death' and its degradation. Texts survive, Derrida tells us, through the breaking down of their meaning and their assimilation into wider linguistic and cultural contexts, even while they resist this biodegradability through the singularity of their existence. Derrida explains that a text 'is on the side of life' because it is 'assimilated [. . .] by a culture that it nourishes, enriches, irrigates, even fecundates,' and this assimilation results in a loss of 'its identity, its figure, or its single signature.' At the same time, however, 'the singularity of a work resists, does not let itself be assimilated, but stays on the surface and survives like an indestructible artefact or in any case one which is less destructible than another.'[24] Texts 'live' and 'survive' in the space between such *biodegradability* and *non-biodegradability*: between the continued preservation of the singularity of their existence and the continuous erosion and corrosion of this identity. What Derrida is referring to here is the general communicability of a text—its ability to transmit meaning and for this meaning to be translated into wider cultural contexts. For a text to have meaning, indeed for it to exist, it must be able to be assimilated into a cultural context through the processes of reading and reception. As Derrida explains it, a text must be able to 'pass into the general culture, into the "life" of "culture" while enriching it with anonymous but nourishing substances.' But this cultural assimilation simultaneously also constitutes an 'annihilation of identity' through which the singularity of the text is itself eroded.[25] The continued existence and survival of a text depends on the preservation of its own singularity—remaining, in some ways, 'inassimilable, indeed unreadable'[26]—as well as the dissolution of this identity through the processes of reading. A text can be said to *survive*, therefore, through its simultaneous *biodegradability* and *non-biodegradability*, and it can only ever *live* by *living on* in its differential relationships with other texts, other environments and other cultural contexts.

Derrida's discussion of the biodegradability and non-biodegradability of texts draws attention to the way that the singularity of a work can only ever exist in the context of a wider cultural environment, and how, ultimately, its continued *survivance* is dependent on its dissolution and assimilation into this environment. We can think of a text's dissemination within a shared cultural sphere: the way that particular tropes or motifs can achieve virality or the way that specific words and phrases can mutate out of a text and survive outside of it. Such an assimilation into wider cultural contexts marks the continued existence, relevance and survival of a work beyond the specific boundaries of its own identity. Indeed, it is in the dissemination and subsequent erosion of such an identity that a text is able to *live on*. The life and survival of any cultural object lies in the possibility of it being read, interpreted and disseminated. As Derrida says of Defoe's *Robinson Crusoe*, a text survives in the processes by which it is 'read and will be read, interpreted, taught, saved, translated, reprinted, illustrated, filmed, kept alive by millions of inheritors.'[27] Michael Naas describes this as 'the self-destruction or self-forgetting of cultural objects, the way in which such objects, after a time of being recalled and identified, simply become part of the white noise of culture itself, of the archive.'[28] '"Biodegradability",' he adds, 'names, first, the effacement of identity, the erasure of a signature, the becoming nonthing of the cultural thing, but then also, and through this annihilation of identity, a survival—albeit an anonymous survival—in the culture more generally.'[29] Biodegradability constitutes a disintegration of the identity of the text as well as the possibility of a broader form of survival that arises out of this disintegration.

It is for this reason that Michael Peterson argues that the relationship between biodegradability and non-biodegradability is not 'a simple binary' but rather 'one of necessary coimplication.'[30] While in his essay Derrida relates the notion of biodegradability to actual cultural objects (masterpieces, books, etc.), Peterson shows how the relationship between biodegradability and non-biodegradability can also be understood more broadly in relation to the workings of the sign or the trace. Peterson returns to Derrida's discussion of the differentiality and iterability of the sign in "Signature Event Context" and notes that 'the language of biodegradability' that appears in the diary fragments 'can be understood as an elaboration of the sense in which a sign engenders new contexts.'[31] 'That a sign can acquire meaning in a radically new context,' Peterson explains, 'is the condition for the transmission of meaning in general. If a sign could not be in-formed and taken up anew in a context that is other than its own, the sign would remain radically idiosyncratic and unable to communicate. That a sign can be read in a new context is a necessary condition for it functioning as a sign at all.'[32] Crucially, this relationship between the sign and the context in which it is taken up is a relationship of intra-activity by which 'the sign itself becomes part of the context in which it is encountered and, in this way, alters the context in which it is encountered.'[33] The context alters the *sign*, but this reception and assimilation in turn also alters the *context*. It is in the space of this intra-activity that Peterson identifies the co-implication of the biodegradability and non-biodegradability of the sign—or what could be better referred to here as its *survivance*. 'That a sign is taken up in new contexts (and so undergoes shifts in meanings and engenders changes in context),' Peterson explains, '*is* its survival.'[34] The survivance of a text or a sign is its simultaneous disintegration *and* survival. Survivance names the effacement of a text *through* its own survival and its survival *through* its own effacement always with and within the environments in which it is received.

As Peterson shows, this survivance is at work in all forms of textuality. The living textuality of a text, a sign or a trace arises out of the entangled processes of biodegradability and non-biodegradability by which it is transformed while, at the same time, also transforming the environments within which it is received. Texts and signs may resist this disseminating biodegradability in their attempts to *mean*, but all meanings, texts and signs can nevertheless only ever exist as a result of such biodegradability, ensuring their dissemination within different contexts.[35] A text or a sign can only ever have meaning if its identity can be dissolved and it can be taken up differently and differentially within its environments. If a text is wholly biodegradable, then it will simply not exist; and if it were absolutely non-biodegradable, then it would be wholly 'insignificant.'[36] As Michael Naas puts it: 'one might hope that a piece of writing not biodegrade, that it remain identifiable, that its signature remain legible, but this can happen only at the price of that writing not being fully assimilated or integrated into culture. And so one might also hope for just the opposite, for a piece of writing to decompose and become part of the general culture, part of its language, its discourses.'[37] It is only through its own movements of disintegration, decomposition and transformation *in and with its environment* that signs, texts and indeed *textuality* itself can live and survive.

Biological Survivance

Derrida's linking of the survival of a text to its entangled biodegradability and non-biodegradability relies on a similar understanding of biological life as being always intimately entangled with otherness. Although, as Derrida notes, the term 'biodegradability' commonly refers to 'an artificial product, most often an industrial product, whenever it lets itself be decomposed by microorganisms' (a point that we will return to shortly),[38] this concept is rooted in a principle of organic decomposition that is most commonly exhibited by biological matter. Derrida's description of texts surviving through a process of cultural or linguistic 'decomposition' thus relies on an understanding of the survival of *biological life* as being involved in material processes of decay and decomposition which entangle living beings in their environments in varied and complex ways. In my reading of the notion of textuality in the previous chapter, and my analysis of how it functions as more than a simple metaphor for the workings of life, I argued that the textuality of biological life is always constituted out of otherness and difference—that it can be recognised in the way that living cells and organisms are composed out of the production and reproduction of difference in inter- and intra-active processes that always implicate them in that which they supposedly are not. We can now begin to see how this biological textuality is also related to questions of biodegradability and survivance. On the level of the cell, but also more broadly in the bodies of living organisms, and in larger assemblages of living beings, the preservation and survival of *life*—the singular existence of an organism, the continued existence of a species or indeed the continued survival of an ecosystem—is intimately entangled in different processes of decay, decomposition and death, to the extent that, in a certain sense, the survival of life can itself be recognised *as* such a decomposition.

Life *lives* through difference, through exchange and through processes of decomposition and recomposition that entangle it in death. In his reading of Jacob's *The Logic of Life* and of Derrida's own analysis of this text in *Life Death*, David Wills argues that 'the logic of life'—the movement of 'replication and replacement, [. . .] repetition and contrived difference' that Derrida identifies as the textual and differential process at work in cellular reproduction—'is both life and death.'[39] Wills makes this remark in the context of a wider discussion of the relationship between sexual and asexual reproduction and the death of an organism.[40] But we can perhaps better understand this entanglement if we think of the ways in which the continued *preservation* and *maintaining* of life is entangled in different processes of death and decomposition. At a cellular level, the continued existence of any organism is dependent on the routine 'killing off' of cells in a process known as *apoptosis* or programmed cell death. Old cells are broken down so as to be reassimilated and absorbed into new structures in what can be thought of as an *internal* nutrient cycle of which death is an integral part. This is complemented by the process of *mitosis*, where a cell replicates and creates new copies of itself.[41] Both of these processes are essential to the healthy life of an organism because on a cellular level the *life* of an organism and its continual renewal necessitates ongoing *death*.[42]

The *survivance* of life—its entangled *biodegradability* and *non-biodegradability*—can be understood in this way: organisms endure, they survive, they live on, in and through such internal processes of death and decomposition. But, crucially, as we have seen, survivance is not simply linked to self-preservation, and it does not simply occur in the context of some isolated or autonomously lived 'life.' The preservation and survival of an individual text, or, in the context of my discussion here, an individual organism, can only ever take place within the large contexts and environments within which these entities are embedded. And it is here that we can begin to see why the intra-activity that Peterson gestures towards in his reading of Derrida's "Biodegradables" is so crucial. The survival of an individual organism can only ever take place within much broader assemblages of life and death in which other living beings *also* live, survive and decompose. An individual organism can only ever preserve and maintain its own life because it is embedded within larger webs of relationships that allow it to intra-actively assimilate elements of its environment into itself while also transforming and changing that environment in turn. And it is of course into this environment that it will itself also eventually be completely assimilated after its own death in order to be recycled, recomposed and reassimilated into new forms of life. The internal cycles of life and death that exist *within* an organism are always entangled in *external* intra-active processes of decomposition and recomposition through which the organism survives and maintains itself, but within which it will also eventually die and decompose. The survivance of individual organisms is dependent on the intra-active entanglements of such internal *and* external processes of life and death, degeneration and renewal. And, crucially, the continued survivance of the life of these broader ecosystems is also composed of such multitudes of entanglements.

These entangled cycles of exchange and transformation, decomposition and recomposition, disintegration and assimilation complexify and problematise any absolute distinction between the 'inside' and the 'outside,' inviting us to reassess our understanding of life and survival. If we shift our perspective away from what Elizabeth Povinelli calls the 'epidermal point of view' that conditions us to view the world in terms of bounded and individuated beings,[43] and we try to relinquish what Anna Lowenhaupt Tsing describes as the tyranny of 'species self-creation stories' that privilege 'cells, organs, organisms [. . . and] species' over assemblages and entanglements,[44] then we can start to see life as a form of exchange by which organisms and environments are always intra-actively entangled in one another. Povinelli observes that 'although to be "life" a living thing must be structurally and functionally compartmentalized from its environment, nothing can remain alive if it is hermetically sealed off.'[45] And if we consider the way in which certain particular forms of life exist and survive, then even this notion of 'compartmentalisation' becomes suspect. In his exploration of the 'entangled life' of fungi, the biologist and writer Merlin Sheldrake describes lichen as the 'places where an organism unravels into an ecosystem and where an ecosystem congeals into an organism.' Lichen, Sheldrake explains, 'flicker between "wholes" and "collections of parts"'; they are 'a product less of their parts than of the exchanges between those parts.'[46] This exemplifies how the processes of exchange, decomposition and recomposition that we are considering here do not simply occur *within* a living organism; they are what *composes* the organism and what sustains life *across* cells, organisms, species and environments.

Viewing life and the living through the paradigms of textuality and survivance can thus allow us to shift our perspective away from supposedly singular, individual and autonomous forms of life, to consider the complex entanglements and processes of intra-activity that occur between and among different lifeforms. And, equally, it can also draw our attention to the way that this survivance is entangled with that of different forms of *non-living* matter. Sheldrake describes how lichen 'mine minerals from rock in a two-fold process known as "weathering",' whereby 'the inanimate mineral mass within rocks is able to cross over into the metabolic cycles of the living.'[47] Mycorrhizal fungi (that is, fungi that grow and live in symbiotic relationships with plants) also engage in similar behaviours. These organisms 'unpack nutrients bound up in rock and decomposing material. [. . .] They are stationed at the entry point of carbon into terrestrial life cycles and stitch the atmosphere into relation with the ground.'[48] The processes engaged in by these organisms exemplify the way that the survivance of life is always enacted out of entangled relationships with biological as well as *non-biological* matter, and it is out of a consideration of such inter- and intra-activity that a better understanding of the possibility of *material survivance* can emerge.

Material Survivance

If we view the world through the diffractive paradigms I am outlining here, what becomes important is not the relative difference and distinction that exists between various kinds of matter or between the processes and phenomena out of which they are composed. Instead, what these diffractive paradigms draw our attention to are the ways in which different forms of matter and different forms of existence and persistence are *entangled* in intra-active processes that implicate them in one another. Returning to the notion of spectrality mentioned earlier in the chapter, we can again think of survivance as *spectral* because it is always formed out of an entanglement with otherness. The survivance of the living involves material exchanges between and among living and non-living forms of matter that cut across the distinctions and the oppositions by which we categorise life. And as a diffractive paradigm, the notion of survivance can *itself* also enact a similar *conceptual* traversal, highlighting how the processes of exchange and decomposition found in non-living, inanimate and non-biological matter can themselves also constitute complex forms of survivance that are different to but still conceptually and materially entangled with the survivance of the living. Derrida's "Biodegradables" essay is significant not just because it reveals how the survivance of a text, or of textuality more generally, might be related to the textuality and continued survivance of *life*; it is significant because it also allows us to see how these complex entangled processes of textuality and survivance might be recognised in the workings of the supposedly inanimate *materiality* of something like a nuclear trace.

This entanglement is signalled by Derrida's use of the term 'biodegradables.' As I have already noted, the notion of biodegradability usually refers to the breaking down of *artificial* objects composed of *non-living* matter, although it derives from the idea of *biological* decomposition and decay. Indeed, as it is used by Derrida, this term draws attention to the way that both living *and* non-living materials can be involved in complex entanglements of survivance. This is signalled specifically through Derrida's use of parentheses, with the terms '(bio)degrade' and '(bio)degradable' appearing with increased frequency as the essay progresses. Peterson notes that these parentheses serve to 'remind us that we should understand this concept not *only* in relation to the scientific-natural world of biologists' but also, of course, in relation to textuality itself.[49] But this bracketing off of the *bio*-logical by Derrida does more than simply link the living to the textual: it also invites a consideration of how *other* material entities degrade within their environments in ways that may not be biological but may still exhibit the complex entanglements of *biodegradability* and *non-biodegradability*—the complex entanglements of *survivance*, in a word—that we are considering here.[50]

This is most clearly exemplified in the radioactivity of nuclear materials. In his diary fragments, Derrida twice uses the example of nuclear waste to supposedly illustrate the principle of 'nonbiodegradability'—or, as it also appears in the text, 'non-(bio)degradability.'[51] Nuclear waste initially seems to represent for Derrida something that would remain singularly intact over time, persisting endlessly in its apparent unwillingness to decompose. As Michael Naas explains it, nuclear waste thus initially seems to function for Derrida as 'the limit case' for the non-biodegradable because it appears to be 'as close to immortal as a product can be.'[52] If something is truly immortal—if it is infinite or eternal, unable to *degrade* or *die* in any way—then, by implication, it would also not be *alive* and could not be said to *survive* in any way, shape or form.[53] But this is not quite the case with radioactive material, as both Naas and Derrida acknowledge. Radioactive materials are *not* immortal; indeed, they may be said to *live* and to *die* in ways that are not biological but that are nevertheless conceptually comparable to (and also materially entangled in) the survivance of biological life. Naas qualifies Derrida's description of nuclear waste as being 'nonbiodegradable' by explaining that this only *appears* to be the case when the half-life of such waste is 'measured against human life and the human measures that must be taken (or not) to deal with it.'[54] And in his own diary fragments, Derrida notes that the '"non(bio)degradable" is always finite.'[55] Nuclear materials may not *bio*degrade in the way that organic matter does (i.e., by being broken down by living microorganisms),[56] but such materials are nevertheless *still* able to transform, decay and decompose in different ways over time. Indeed, the very *persistence* of nuclear waste—and, as we shall see, of the radioactive isotopes that are embedded in the strata of the earth in what is interpreted and read as a signature or sign of the Anthropocene—*is* such decay and degeneration. As Peterson notes, the 'apparent nonbiodegradability' of nuclear waste 'cannot be thought merely as the continued existence of inert matter': 'nuclear waste lives not *in spite* of its half-life, its slow decay, but precisely *because* of this decay.'[57]

Derrida notes that while nuclear waste might at first appear to pose a limit to the notion of (bio)degradability (and the implication here is of course that it would also constitute a limit case for *survivance*), the very existence of any such limit remains questionable. Derrida suggests that it is at this very point—at the point at which the limit between the (bio)degradable and the non(bio)degradable breaks down—that everything we think we know about existence will also need to be questioned. In a rather cryptic note in which the relative (bio)degradability and non(bio)degradability of nuclear waste becomes linked to the question of metaphor discussed earlier in this chapter and in Chapter 2, Derrida writes: 'If there were a limit [. . .] between the (bio)degradable and the non(bio)degradable, as between the literal and the figurative meaning, this is where it would lie. But I am not sure it does in all strictness. Take up everything again: *physis*, earth, world, man, life, survival, spirit, OK, OK . . . . [. . .].'[58] The possibility of something like the material survivance of nuclear waste (and, as we shall see, of the nuclear *trace*) here also opens up a questioning of the boundary between literal and figurative uses of language—between, that is, the metaphoric and the non-metaphoric, or the 'more than' metaphoric, as discussed earlier—and a questioning of the nature of existence itself in all of its possible permutations.

It is such a questioning that my analysis has been engaged in. The forms of textual and biological survivance that I have been discussing in this chapter are all constituted out of entanglements of preservation and disintegration, decomposition and recomposition, life and death, that cut across different kinds of matter, different forms of life and the different discursive and conceptual paradigms by which we understand these categories. Nuclear material is not *literally* 'alive' in the way that a biological organism is, and it is not *literally* 'textual' in the way that linguistic objects are. But neither are these terms being used here in a *metaphorical* manner. As I continue to show in more detail in the following chapter, in its own movements and processes of transformation, a radioactive isotope enacts forms of material survivance that are not just *conceptually comparable to* but also *materially entangled in* the survivance of other biological and discursive processes. Being attentive to these multiple forms of survivance as they inscribe themselves across different material, living and textual realities can allow us to better understand how these realities are always entangled in one another, interrupting, reworking, transforming and being transformed through their inter- and intra-active relationships. Such an awareness of this diffractive intra-activity can provide us with the tools needed to 'read' something like the so-called radioactive 'signatures' of the Anthropocene *differently*, *differentially* and *diffractively*.

Notes

1. Karen Barad, *Meeting the Universe Halfway: Quantum Physics and the Entanglement of Matter and Meaning* (Durham, NC: Duke University Press, 2007), 72.

2. As will become clearer through the course of my analysis, these two diffractive paradigms supplement one another in ways that cut across the boundaries between text, life and matter.

3. Jacques Derrida, "Des Tours de Babel," in *Difference in Translation*, trans. Joseph F. Graham, ed. Joseph F. Graham (Ithaca, NY: Cornell University Press, 1985), 175.

4. Derrida, "Babel," 178. Discussing the relationship between a literary text and its translation into other languages, Benjamin explains that such texts share a 'natural [. . .], or more specifically, a vital' connection with one another. A translation, Benjamin notes, 'issues from the original—not so much from its life as from its afterlife.' Translation marks a 'stage of continued life'; it is a stage in the continued 'survival' of a text beyond the moment of its initial creation (Walter Benjamin, "The Task of the Translator," in *Walter Benjamin Selected Writings*, Vol. 1, trans. Harry Zohn, ed. Marcus Bullock and Michael W. Jennings (Cambridge, MA: Harvard University Press, 1996), 254, 255).

5. Benjamin himself clearly states that 'the idea of life and afterlife in works of art should be regarded with an entirely unmetaphorical objectivity' ("Task of the Translator," 254).

6. Derrida, "Babel," 178.

7. Christopher Johnson, *System and Writing in the Philosophy of Jacques Derrida* (Cambridge: Cambridge University Press, 1993), 194.

8. Derrida uses the French translation of Benjamin's essay by Maurice de Gandillac in *Mythe et Violence* (Paris: Denoël, 1971).

9. In Harry Zohn's translation of Benjamin's essay into English, 'Überleben' is translated as 'afterlife' (Benjamin, "Task of the Translator," 254), while in a 1997 translation by Steven Randall, both the terms 'afterlife' and 'survival' are used (Walter Benjamin, "The Translator's Task," trans. Steven Rendall, *TTR: traduction, terminologie, rédaction* 10, no. 2 (1997): 151–65).

10. Derrida, "Babel," 206, trans. note.

11. Derrida, "Babel," 178–79.

12. David Wills, *Inanimation: Theories of Inorganic Life* (Minneapolis: University of Minnesota Press, 2016), 167.

13. In his reading of Benjamin's text, Wills interprets the idea of translation broadly, describing it as the 'readerly and, as it were, spectatorial space of a work of literature' through which a text is read, interpreted and commented on (Wills, *Inanimation*, 165). Wills explains that criticism, commentary and translation are all 'forms of exegetical explanation or interruption that [. . .] cause a work to live on otherwise' (Wills, *Inanimation*, 167). Although Wills relates this 'living on' to exegetical texts—to texts that add themselves onto an original through their commentary or criticism—as I show in what follows, every text and all forms of textuality can be said to 'live' in this way. As Derrida argues in *Demeure*, 'before coming to writing, literature depends on reading and the right conferred on it by the experience of reading' (Jacques Derrida, *Demeure: Fiction and Testimony*, trans. Elizabeth Rottenberg (Stanford, CA: Stanford University Press, 2000), 29). A text lives in its readings, its interpretations, its translations and its assimilation into a wider cultural sphere, and therefore the 'life' of a text—whether that of a translation or of an original—must always constitute some form of 'living on.'

14. Derrida, "Babel," 206, trans. note.

15. For more on this see Wills's *Inanimation*.

16. Jacques Derrida, *The Beast and the Sovereign*, Vol. 2, trans. Geoffrey Bennington (Chicago: University of Chicago Press, 2011), 130–31.

17. Derrida, *Beast and Sovereign*, Vol. 2, 131.

18. Jacques Derrida, "Biodegradables: Seven Diary Fragments," in *Signature Derrida*, trans. Peggy Kamuf, ed. Jay Williams (Chicago: University of Chicago Press, 2013).

19. Derrida, "Biodegradables," 155.

20. Derrida, "Biodegradables," 153–54.

21. Derrida, "Biodegradables," 155–56.

22. The two concepts of survivance and biodegradability are, as we shall see very shortly, intimately linked to one another.

23. Derrida, "Biodegradables," 156, 154, 164.

24. Derrida, "Biodegradables," 165.

25. Derrida, "Biodegradables," 180.

26. Derrida, "Biodegradables," 165.

27. Derrida, *Beast and Sovereign*, Vol. 2, 130. This is why, as Derrida explains in *The Beast and the Sovereign*, Vol. 2, the survival of a text is always the survival 'of the *living dead*' (130; emphasis added).

28. Michael Naas, "E-Phemera: Of Deconstruction, Biodegradability, and Nuclear War," in *Eco-Deconstruction: Derrida and Environmental Philosophy*, ed. Matthias Fritsch, Philippe Lynes, and David Wood (New York: Fordham University Press, 2018), 195.

29. Naas, "E-Phemera," 196.

30. Michael Peterson, "Responsibility and the Non(bio)degradable," in *Eco-Deconstruction*, Fritsch, Lynes, and Wood, 255.

31. Peterson, "Responsibility," 255.

32. Peterson, "Responsibility," 254–55.

33. Peterson, "Responsibility," 254–55.

34. Peterson, "Responsibility," 256.

35. Derrida appears to draw a distinction between 'the work' as he discusses it in "Biodegradables" and textuality more generally, explaining that 'in the manner of a proper name, the work is singular; it does not function like an ordinary element of natural language in its everyday usage. That is why it lets itself be assimilated less easily by culture to whose institution it nevertheless contributes' (Derrida, "Biodegradables," 165). But, as Peterson's analysis suggests, the distinction here is one of a *relative* biodegradability/non-biodegradability—a distinction made along a scale of survivance, so to speak, that is operable in all forms of text.

36. Derrida, "Biodegradables," 165. Derrida explains that the incommunicable elements of a text—what remains untranslatable and untransferable—are what resist assimilation and erosion; but they are also what prevents a text from living and surviving. In protecting its own singularity, a text remains 'inassimilable'; it may 'survive a long time' by resisting erosion, but it may also consequently be unable to achieve cultural longevity (Derrida, "Biodegradables," 165–73).

37. Naas, "E-Phemera," 196–97.

38. Derrida, "Biodegradables," 153.

39. Wills, *Inanimation*, 16.

40. In *The Logic of Life*, Jacob links death to the emergence of sexual reproduction, arguing that in the case of the asexual reproduction of an organism such as a bacterium, there is no real death. The original 'parent' cell may cease to exist, but it does so only through the process of replication by which it splits into two new 'daughter' cells. This distinction between what Jacob calls 'contingent death' and death itself (as cited by Wills, *Inanimation*, 14) is deconstructed by both Derrida and David Wills (see *Life Death*, 106–14; and *Inanimation*, 14–15). As Wills argues in the context of this discussion, life (regardless of the form that it takes) is always a form of 'life in death or death in life or lifedeath' (*Inanimation*, 15).

41. In order for a cell to reproduce, the two strands of DNA contained in the nucleus must be torn apart and used as templates for the creation of new corresponding strands. It is this that allows a cell to divide into new daughter cells—either two cells that are identical to the first, as in the reproduction of regular somatic or bodily cells in cellular renewal (mitosis) and in the reproduction of single-celled organisms such as bacteria—or into the four genetically distinct gametes produced through meiosis for sexual reproduction.

42. As a leading biology textbook puts it, cell death 'plays a key role both in embryonic development and in adult tissues' (Geoffrey M. Cooper, *The Cell: A Molecular Approach*, 8th ed. (Oxford: Oxford University Press, 2019), 637).

43. Elizabeth A. Povinelli, *Geontologies: A Requiem to Late Capitalism* (Durham, NC: Duke University Press, 2016), 40.

44. Anna Lowenhaupt Tsing, *The Mushroom at the End of the World: On the Possibility of Life in Capitalist Ruins* (Princeton, NJ: Princeton University Press, 2017), 140.

45. Povinelli, *Geontologies*, 43.

46. Merlin Sheldrake, *Entangled Life: How Fungi Make Our Worlds, Change Our Minds, and Shape Our Futures* (London: The Bodley Head, 2020), 99. Emphasising the kinds of exchanges between organisms, species and living and non-living matter that I am discussing here, Sheldrake explains that 'a portion of the minerals in your body is likely to have passed through a lichen at some point' (*Entangled Life*, 85).

47. Sheldrake, *Entangled Life*, 85.

48. Sheldrake, *Entangled Life*, 142.

49. Peterson, "Responsibility," 255.

50. The parentheses blur the distinction between biological decomposition (the decomposition of biological matter by living microorganisms), biodegradation proper (where organic 'products' of human industry are broken down by living microorganisms) and the possible breakdown of other forms of inorganic matter by both biological and non-biological means. Discussing her own use of the term 'biodegradation,' Jennifer Gabrys explains that 'bio' need not be understood as referring to a material's own capacity for organic decay: inorganic materials might also be said to biodegrade because the processes of erosion and degradation by which they break down into smaller particles can be entangled with biological life, whether directly or indirectly. Discussing the biodegradability of plastics, for instance, Gabrys suggests that such a reading of the term can help us think 'the forms of life—the organisms, processes and environments—that are drawn into the ongoing breakdown of plastics, whether by inadvertently ingesting microplastics or undergoing increased exposure to pollutants that are concentrated on plastic debris surfaces' (Jennifer Gabrys, "Plastic and the Work of the Biodegradable," in *Accumulation: The Material Politics of Plastic*, ed. Jennifer Gabrys, Gay Hawkins, and Mike Michael (London: Routledge, 2013), 211). As Bastian and van Dooren similarly argue, what is so 'compelling' about these supposedly non(bio)degradable materials is 'not simply their incredible endurance over time, but the particular ways in which these entities become bound up with, intersect with, others' life processes and possibilities—for good or ill, often a bit of both'

(Michelle Bastian and Thom van Dooren, "Editorial Preface: The New Immortals: Immortality and Infinitude in the Anthropocene," *Environmental Philosophy* 14, no. 1 (Spring 2017): 4, https://doi.org/10.5840/envirophil20171411).

51. Derrida, "Biodegradables," 159, 207. Derrida here extends his orthographic play, describing nuclear waste as 'non(bio)degradable' (207), in a way that further complexifies his discussion. Depending on how it is read, this term could be taken to mean that which does not biodegrade (i.e., that which does not degrade through biological means but can break down in some other way), or it could also mean that which does not degrade, period, by any means whatsoever.

52. Naas, "E-Phemera," 193, 201.

53. Martin Hägglund argues that there is a clear distinction between 'survival' on the one hand and 'immortality' on the other. Hägglund explains that the two concepts are incompatible because the continued survival of life requires death, and it is precisely such death that is absent from immortal existence. '[T]he state of immortality,' Hägglund explains, 'would annihilate every form of survival, since it would annihilate the time of mortal life' (Martin Hägglund, *Radical Atheism: Derrida and the Time of Life* (Stanford, CA: Stanford University Press, 2008), 2). If, as we have seen, biological processes of life are intimately entangled with death—if, indeed, life requires death to survive—then an immortality that persists and never dies cannot constitute a form of life or any comparable form of survival. This can be related to the states of preserved stasis discussed in Chapter 1. Although cryopreservation practices are intended to protect, preserve and extend life through what Patricia MacCormack calls 'techniques of immortality' (Patricia MacCormack, *The Ahuman Manifesto: Activism for the End of the Anthropocene* (London: Bloomsbury, 2020), 70), what these facilities actually house are forms of interrupted and suspended life. As Matthew Chrulew puts it, cryopreservation facilities 'secure life against living itself' (Matthew Chrulew, "Freezing the Ark: The Cryopolitics of Endangered Species Preservation," in *Cryopolitics: Frozen Life in a Melting World*, ed. Joanna Radin and Emma Kowal (Cambridge, MA: MIT Press, 2017), 299).

54. Naas, "E-Phemera," 201. Joseph Masco makes a similar point: 'from a human perspective,' he tells us, nuclear waste is 'virtually eternal' (Joseph Masco, *The Nuclear Borderlands: The Manhattan Project in Post–Cold War New Mexico* (Princeton, NJ: Princeton University Press, 2006), 30). Nuclear waste can contain elements such as cesium-137, strontium-90 or plutonium-239. While cesium-137 and strontium-90 have half-lives of around thirty years (meaning that roughly half of the radioactive isotopes will have decayed in thirty years), plutonium-239 has a half-life of twenty-four thousand years.

55. Derrida, "Biodegradables," 198.

56. As we shall see in Chapter 4, however, some radioactive materials can indeed be broken down in somewhat comparable ways by certain microorganisms. In fact, practices of 'bioremediation' are based on this principle.

57. Peterson, "Responsibility," 250, 256.

58. Derrida, "Biodegradables," 207–8 (square brackets in text).

CHAPTER FOUR

∿

Rereading the Nuclear Trace

Diffractive Paradigms for the Anthropocene

The Anthropocene Working Group (AWG)—the official group tasked with assessing the validity of the Anthropocene as a geological and stratigraphic time unit—has identified radioactive isotopes deposited in rock sediments after the fallout from nuclear weapons testing in the 1950s as the 'trace' in the strata of the earth that is most likely to function as the 'primary marker' of the Anthropocene in the distant future.[1] The AWG's categorisation of radionuclide deposits as future stratigraphic markers of the present is based on a semiotic reading of these geochemical phenomena as constituting would-be signs or signals of a past human epoch.[2] Such a reading is fundamental to many scientific and cultural discourses on the Anthropocene that retrospectively view the present from the vantage point of a supposedly unknown future while simultaneously also projecting the anthropocentric values and assumptions of the present onto this future. As I have shown in earlier chapters, this circular and specular logic works to affirm the significance of the present world, even while it appears to contemplate its demise. In an effort to resist the anthropocentric baggage that such a semiotic reading of the Anthropocene carries with it, I have proposed a different understanding of the lithic trace—one that focuses on the *material textuality* of such geochemical phenomena and the rich and complex networks of intra-activity out of which they are composed. Read through the paradigms of textuality and survivance conceptualised in previous chapters, these traces appear not as semiotic signs that point back to the past but as material inscriptions that survive in their intra-active entanglements with other material, biological and discursive phenomena.

The assumption that radioactive traces in the strata of the earth will, in the future, function as clear signs or signatures of human activity in the Anthropocene is predicated on the fact that many nuclear isotopes are not commonly found in nature and are the product of human synthesis. The existence of these isotopes seems to clearly point to the presence of human beings upon the earth, serving as proof that, as Elizabeth Kolbert puts it, 'something extraordinary happened at the moment in time that counts for us as today.'[3] But the fact that something is human-*made* does not mean that it automatically also constitutes a human *sign*. To assume that radioactive isotopes inherently constitute a mark of human presence—that they are a signature that 'uniquely conveys the former presence of its author; a mark that remains, and remains meaningful, in the absence of the signatory'[4]—is to project a very specific human representational framework onto an entity that exceeds, and by its very nature will *outlive*, any such representation.[5] A semiotic reading of the anthropocenic trace hinges on the assumption that such marks of difference have value when they function as signs that have meaning—that they are endowed with significance because they are able to direct us to a point of origin that exists outside of themselves. But such meaning can only ever exist as a result of complex processes and movements of differentiation that also manifest themselves otherwise—in different forms of textuality and survivance that are not primarily linguistic or semiotic but *material*. A consideration of these other textualities and movements of survivance can reveal forms of *non-human* inscription that share a diffractive relationship with human language and discourse—forms of inscription that can and should be recognised as having 'significance' even though they may not *signify* anything at all.

This chapter continues to explore the possibility of engaging in a material 'rereading' of the lithic trace through an analysis of the radioactivity of nuclear isotopes. Using the paradigms of textuality and survivance developed in earlier chapters, I show how radionuclides embedded in the strata of the earth can be described as 'inscriptions' that write themselves into existence in the intra-active entanglements through which they 'survive,' or even 'live' and 'live on.' As my previous discussions of metaphor would suggest, such descriptions of the 'inscriptions' and the 'life' of these radionuclides are not merely metaphorical; they operate in a way that diffractively recognises the entanglement of these radioactive isotopes and their survivance in the strata with and within many other biological and discursive processes, practices and phenomena. A recognition of this diffractivity and entanglement invites us to think these radioactive traces not as human signs that point back to the past in a way that affirms the value and the significance of the human within it but as entities that enact complex assemblages of intra-activity of which the human is but one part. Such thinking allows us to see how all human, biological and material realities are entangled in one another, composed out of complex assemblages of intra-activity that challenge traditional notions of agency, causality, identity and presence.

Spectral Inscriptions

My exploration of the material textuality of radioactive isotopes begins with the work of a number of critics who analyse how video footage and photographs taken in Chernobyl after the 1986 disaster display particular marks and traces of nuclear radiation and contamination. Discussing a series of photographs taken by the radiation monitor Aleksandr Kupny inside the ruins of the destroyed Reactor No. 4, the historian Kate Brown explains that the photos display 'tiny orange flecks and flashing lights'—a 'snowfall of tiny crystalline flakes that float through every scene of silent ruin.' Brown describes these marks as a form of *self-portraiture* created by the 'multitude of photons of radioactive energy' that swarmed around Kupny 'as he pressed his shutter button.' Significantly, she notes that these 'points of light' are not mere 'representations'—images of something that exists *outside* of the photograph—but forms of 'energy embodied.'[6] The 'decaying isotopes' that Kupny and his camera encountered in the destroyed chambers of the reactor '*are* the raw material of his photography,' and it is the direct material inscription of these isotopes that is captured on film.[7] Susan Schuppli makes a similar claim in a discussion of video footage taken by the Ukrainian filmmaker Vladimir Shevchenko in Chernobyl. Schuppli argues that 'the disaster *inscribed itself* directly into the emulsive layer of the film as decaying radioactive particles transgressed the exterior casing of the movie camera,' creating not merely an *image* of radioactivity but a direct material trace of it.[8]

Schuppli distinguishes between images of nuclear disasters that merely *represent* the effects of a nuclear bomb, such as the iconic photographs of mushroom clouds that depict the immediate aftermath of a nuclear explosion, and the 'amorphous contagion' of these radioactive isotopes leaving their mark on these filmic surfaces.[9] While the *image* of a mushroom cloud 'separates the visual field from the material conditions that it documents,' providing a pictorial representation of an external 'reality,' the radioactive marks on these filmic substrates are *materially* implicated in the realities they capture.[10] In Shevchenko's recordings, Schuppli explains, film no longer merely functions as an 'indexical trace'—as a 'record and index of past events.' Instead, it 'collapse[s] the gap between representation and the real, form and content, signification and affect' and 'enter[s] into a feedback loop with the *actual* material residue of the world.'[11] These forms of textual inscription, Schuppli's analysis suggests, cannot simply be understood *semiotically*, as signs that point to some external reality; they constitute an altogether *other* form of geochemical and material inscription that, in the context of these films and photographs, becomes entangled with human forms of visual representation.

The analyses of these marks of radiation and radioactivity on film are important because they illustrate how radionuclides in the earth's strata can also be read as material forms of textual inscription that write themselves into existence. Brown draws a parallel between the marks on Kupny's photographs and the radioactive isotopes in the earth's strata, arguing that the radionuclides that inscribed themselves onto Kupny's film at Chernobyl are 'the same decaying particles' that 'geologists will locate in sedimentary rock and soil [. . .] still beating strongly thousands of years from now.'[12] These radionuclides may be read by present and future geologists as signs or signatures of an anthropocenic present-made-past, but beyond this semiotic interpretation and the human forms of reading that it presupposes, they may also be 'read' differently—as material inscriptions whose textuality is constituted out of the chemical processes by which they inter- and intra-act with and within their environments. Like the marks on film, these stratal inscriptions do not merely point to some external past event, and they cannot simply be defined with reference to a single and solely human point of origin. As both Schuppli and Brown make clear, the traces of radioactivity and radiation recorded on Kupny's and Shevchenko's photographs and films should be thought of as the inscriptions of radioactive isotopes *writing themselves* into and onto these substrates through their continued decay. These are *non-human* forms of textuality that are composed out of complex chemical and material processes of survivance.

The textuality of these radioactive isotopes is linked by Brown and Schuppli to the 'life' of radioactive matter. Although nuclear materials are not biological, and thus cannot be said to *live* in the way that organisms do, these radionuclides are nevertheless repeatedly referred to by these critics as being *alive* in some comparable way. Schuppli describes the traces of radioactivity left behind on Shevchenko's film as 'dangerously alive,'[13] while Brown notes that 'when, in the nuclear power plant, Soviet engineers created isotopes not found in nature—strontium, cesium, plutonium—these isotopes, once born, continued living their own "life," following the "natural" properties of radioactive decay.'[14] Joseph Masco makes a similar claim when discussing the unstable nature of plutonium. This element, he notes, is 'not unlike a strange new life form, [. . .] always evolving, changing in appearance.'[15]

Significantly, these critics also link the so-called life of radioactive isotopes to something *ghostly* and *spectral*. Masco relates the 'lives,' or better still, the *half-lives*, of nuclear materials and their biological, social and cultural effects to the Freudian uncanny: to a sensibility that is associated, in part, with the figure of the ghost and a blurring of 'the distinction between the living and the dead.'[16] Schuppli uses similar spectral imagery: she describes Shevchenko's film as being haunted by 'radioactive ghosts' that create a 'pyrotechnics of syncopated spectrality' when the damaged film footage is played.[17] And Brown describes the photographs taken by Kupny in the inner chambers of Chernobyl's so-called sarcophagus—a term that itself conjures up images of death, burial and possible afterlife—as similarly 'haunting' in their capturing of the spectral lives and afterlives of these radioactive isotopes.[18]

The spectral and the ghostly are typically associated with the possibility of something continuing to *live on* beyond the end of life—of something remaining present after its apparent death. Ghosts occupy a space *after* life, a state that *follows on* from life while being neither fully living nor fully dead. It is in the space of the continued presence of that which is supposed to be absent (and simultaneously, therefore, the absence of that which remains present) that the experience of the spectral generally unfolds. Such a spectrality appears to point back to a previous life, referring to what once was, and, in this sense, it functions as a *sign* or a *trace* of the past. The ghost *lives on*—but only as a remnant of what was once alive, persisting on the boundary between absence and presence, present and past, life and death. But the spectral 'life' of radioactive materials is not quite lived in this way. Radioactive isotopes *live on* as the traces of a past event, certainly—traces of a nuclear explosion, for instance, and its fallout. But this *living on* constitutes a form of survivance that does far more than simply point back to the past. As Karen Barad notes in a discussion of the nuclear entanglements of past and present, hauntings are not 'mere recollections or reverberations of what was.'[19] The radioactive isotopes that are inscribed in the strata of the earth are not spectral merely because they constitute the ghostly traces and remnants of a past nuclear event, or because they can function as the signs or signatures of a past human world that remains present through its ghostly inscriptions in the earth's strata. Instead, these radionuclides 'live on' through their own *material forms of survivance* and their *inscription* and *entanglement* in the myriad forms of living and non-living matter that they intersect with.

We can return here to the discussions of spectrality engaged in in earlier chapters, where the spectral was described not simply in terms of an absence that remains present, or a presence that remains absent (a life, for instance, that no longer *lives* but that somehow continues to *live on* through ghostly haunting), but was related to the way that presence (in every possible sense of the term) is always constituted out of otherness, always haunted by the movements of difference and *différance* that allow for continued existence. Every form of existence, every persistence, every *living on*, is spectral because it is constituted out of otherness.[20] The nuclear trace is no different: it lives and survives *hauntologically*,[21] blurring 'the distinction between the animate and the inanimate'[22] and traversing the boundaries between different forms of matter, always transforming itself intra-actively through these entanglements. Radioactive materials 'age,' Masco explains, in an 'uncontainable' way, and they 'execute their own uncanny form of manifest destiny, traveling an unpredictable course through ecosystems and bodies, creating new social and biological beings.'[23] The 'life' and survivance of radioactive materials consists of the processes of radioactive decay by which they transform into different states while in turn also transforming the bodies and environments they come into contact with. These materials *live* and *live on* spectrally through these intra-active transformations.

Radioactive Survivance

Building on the notion of a spectral 'life' of radioactivity, Masco describes how scientists working at the nuclear facilities in Los Alamos in the United States use particular biological and bodily 'metaphors' in their descriptions of nuclear materials and nuclear bombs.[24] Siegfried S. Hecker and Joseph C. Martz, for instance, describe the chemical transformations of nuclear materials as a form of 'aging,' arguing that radioactive isotopes age 'from the outside in' as a result of interactions with their environment, and 'from the inside out' through radioactive decay.[25] Nuclear bombs are consequently perceived and treated by scientists as having biological bodies that can be 'exposed to the elements' and become 'increasingly infirm' with age. These weapons are said to receive 'gerontological' care to manage and mitigate these changes: they undergo 'check-ups' and 'hospital' visits, and they 'retire' and are given post-mortem 'autopsies.'[26] Although radioactive materials do not live and age according to any conceivable *biological* definition of these terms, these descriptions suggest that there is nevertheless something that *survives* in radioactivity, something that connects it to the textual and differential processes of reproduction, evolution, life and death as they manifest themselves in living cells, organisms and assemblages. Nuclear materials are not composed of DNA molecules or biological cells that replicate and reproduce,[27] mutate and die; they do not preserve themselves through processes of cellular renewal and cell death, and their aging is not a result of changes and mutations in these processes. But there are *other* mutations, *other* forms of decomposition and recomposition at work in the chemical transformations of such materials—complex and entangled interactions of preservation and assimilation through which radioactive isotopes survive and decay, acting on and being acted upon by other forms of living and non-living matter—that are somehow related to the workings of biological life.

In the previous chapter I explored how the diffractive paradigm of *survivance* can allow us to see that the continued existence of certain non-biological forms of matter, such as that of radioactive materials, is wrought out of entangled movements and processes of biodegradability and non-biodegradability, preservation and decay, that are conceptually related to and materially implicated in the processes of life and death in biological organisms and the survival of textual entities within a cultural sphere.[28] Masco refers to the terms used by the Los Alamos scientists as 'metaphors'—tropes that create a conceptual and rhetorical relationship between things that remain materially distinct from one another. But what we have here is not just a comparison or a simple metaphor. The differences that allow us to distinguish between the biological and the material are also what entangle these different realities in one another. Survivance marks the material movements *between* and *amongst* these realities and the different phenomena that comprise them. The survivance of material entities, biological organisms and textual objects is constituted out of the relationships that these entities have with their environments, relationships through which supposedly singular individual entities are transformed, while also transforming these environments in turn. As we shall see, such intra-active transformations have complex cascading effects that ripple across broader ecological, material and social and cultural realities in ways that materially connect these realities together. Tracking the spectral life and survivance of something like a nuclear isotope requires that one follow the contours of these intra-active transformations and 'read' them in all of their dizzying complexity.

Radioactive isotopes are unstable, which means that they decay into other states, emitting alpha particles, beta particles or gamma rays into their environments. Plutonium, for instance, decays into uranium and alpha particles (helium nuclei) which transfer energy to the electrons and atoms in their surroundings. This results in the irradiation of surrounding molecules, which break down as a result, as well as in the self-irradiation of other remaining plutonium isotopes.[29] These processes affect the immediate environments within which the radioactive material is embedded—such as the geochemical composition of soil and rock sediments or the biochemistry of the cells of an organism in cases where radioactive isotopes are absorbed, ingested or inhaled.[30] But the transformations do not end there. Such changes to the environment can also have an effect on the remaining isotopes, because radionuclides are themselves also influenced by certain environmental factors and possible changes to them. Radioactive isotopes are involved in chemical and biochemical reactions that involve sorption, oxidation, reduction and complexation; they interact with minerals and organic molecules in soil and rock, and they are acted upon by certain microorganisms with which they also interact in turn.[31] These are processes of decomposition, recomposition, assimilation and absorption by which radionuclides lose or gain electrons, become more or less soluble, form bonds with organic and inorganic substances, diffuse into rock substrates, are incorporated into minerals and become attached to cell membranes or bind with biomolecules that can be absorbed into living cells.[32] These changes can alter the behaviour of these isotopes in their environments, in that they can affect their solubility and mobility, influence their concentration in groundwater and make it more or less likely for them to be transported to new areas and new environments where they will continue to decay and engage in such inter- and intra-active processes of transformation.[33]

Radioactive materials *survive* through their decay with and within their environments; they *live* and *live on* through these entangled processes of survivance that transform both them and their environments in turn. It is worth recalling here Michael Peterson's reflections on the biodegradability and non-biodegradability of the sign, referred to in my discussion of textual and biological survivance in Chapter 3. In his reading of Derrida's "Biodegradables," Peterson notes that a sign is transformed as it is assimilated into its environment, but it also transforms this environment in turn.[34] The survivance of biological organisms follows a similar pattern: biological exchanges within and amongst organisms in any given environment will change that environment in ways that can consequently also transform the lives of the organisms within it. Whether we consider the reception, assimilation and survival of a text through the contexts of its reading, the continued preservation of living organisms within larger ecosystems, or, indeed, as we can see here, the survivance of radioactive isotopes in different environmental contexts, what becomes significant is the way that these processes are never isolated or self-contained but always cut across the boundaries between individual entities and phenomena, entangling them in one another. And the environment in which an entity is received and within which it interacts—be it material, geochemical, biological or semiotic—is *itself* always also reactive, degradable, assimilable and adaptable. This means that such interactions always *intra*-actively feed back into one another,[35] producing new entanglements, new forms of assimilation and new manifestations of survivance that cut across different forms of life, matter and discourse.

The concept of mutation, as it is used by Joseph Masco, can help illustrate the significance of such intra-active entanglements. Masco compares the decay of radioactive materials to the evolution of a biological lifeform[36]—to something that *mutates*, transforming and evolving into something new. But he also mobilises this concept to analyse the wide-ranging biological, ecological, scientific, militaristic, social, cultural, economic, political, geographic and psychological effects of the US nuclear complex, showing the far-reaching impact that nuclear radiation can have on different biological, ecological and social realities.[37] The concept of mutation is useful because it draws attention to how such processes and phenomena are always entangled in one another, how they continue to evolve over time, and how these evolutions can themselves lead to further mutations and adaptations in continuing cycles of change and transformation that feed into one another. In biology, mutations are said to occur when parts of a DNA molecule are incorrectly 'copied' during replication, resulting in changes to the genetic makeup of a cell. As the field of epigenetics evidences, and as the effects of nuclear radiation themselves also make clear,[38] such genetic mutations are often the product of complex intra-active biochemical entanglements between living organisms and their material environments that affect the genetic makeup of an individual organism. These changes can have a direct impact on the lived reality of that organism, but they can also have wider and more far-reaching effects. They may be carried into the germ line, thus affecting the lives of other organisms of the same species, and they may also influence other species by indirectly causing other changes within an ecosystem. The chemical 'evolution' and 'mutation' of a radioactive isotope, as it is conceptualised by Masco—that is, the transformation of a radionuclide as it survives and decays into new states, emitting radiation into its environment—has these same ripple effects. The 'mutation' of radioactive decay can cause other mutations in living organisms that themselves set in motion complex biological, ecological and environmental intra-actions that have further cascading effects on other organisms and wider ecosystems.

In animals, for instance, exposure to radiation through the ingestion, inhalation or absorption of radioactive particles from contaminated environments can disrupt processes of DNA replication and cell renewal, leading to genetic mutations that cause broader physical changes, such as cancer, organ damage and impaired immunity.[39] It can also cause irregularities in the animal's reproductive system and possible abnormalities in offspring.[40] If the mutations are passed down through the germ line as hereditary traits, then they can lead to other possible evolutionary adaptations and species transformations over time.[41] Changes to species diversity and productivity, and wider species adaptations,[42] can affect the relationships between different groups of organisms by disrupting predator-prey relationships,[43] or productive inter-species assemblages—such as those between pollinators, plants and birds that disperse seeds.[44] The impact on such ecological relationships can create further environmental stressors or increased resources and set in motion cascades of other intra-active biological and ecological mutations and transformations that continue to occur over time. As Stanislav A. Geras'kin notes, 'the changes observed in an ecosystem after irradiations are caused not only by radiation per se, but also by the inherent interactions between species.'[45] These interactions move back and forth between different organisms, species and the environmental phenomena they are entangled with, each *influencing* and being in turn *influenced by* these collective mutations.

For Masco, what is at stake in the concept of mutation is 'a transformation that is reproduced generationally, making the mutation a specific kind of break with the past that reinvents the future.'[46] Mutations are 'multi-generational'—they are forms of change that will 'continue to proliferate, promising unpredictable outcomes' over time.[47] But such mutations are not merely multi- or inter-*generational*; they do not simply cut across different generations of living organisms. If we think of radioactive decay as a form of mutation *in itself*, then we can see how the kinds of mutations being discussed here actually cut across different forms of *matter* as well as different ecological realities and different forms of life. What the concept of mutation allows us to see is how the survivance of a radioactive isotope and the radiation it produces are entangled with the survivance of many other material, biological, ecological as well as social and discursive entities in ways that are always *inter-material*. As Masco's own analysis evidences, the decay of a radioactive isotope and the genetic changes it can create in organisms and species[48] are always entangled with many other biological and non-biological 'mutations.' These can include changes to ecological environments as well as changing social, political and discursive practices and phenomena that intra-act with one another in ever-evolving and entangled cascades of change and transformation.

Rereading Chernobyl

Clear examples of such *inter-material* intra-actions and entanglements can be found in the ecological, environmental, political and social transformations that resulted from the many different nuclear explosions and disasters that have occurred across the world since the 1940s. The accident that occurred at the Chernobyl Nuclear Power Plant in April 1986 is particularly significant in the context of my argument because Chernobyl is often perceived as a 'test case' for the Anthropocene—it is viewed and described as an example of what might be left of the earth following the possible extinction of the human species. In *The World Without Us*, for instance, Alan Weisman argues that 'in a world without humans the plants and animals we leave behind will have to deal with many more Chernobyls,'[49] and in his *Notes from an Apocalypse* Mark O'Connell describes the 'postapocalyptic wasteland' of the Chernobyl Exclusion Zone as a 'fully interactive virtual rendering of a world to come'—one that allows the author to 'see the end of the world from the vantage point of its aftermath.'[50] Chernobyl functions for O'Connell as both a trace of the past and an indication of what the future might hold, an example of how the entire earth might be reduced to a mere remnant of a lost past, serving as no more than a ghostly trace of what once was. In this sense, Chernobyl functions as a *sign* that itself points to how the earth as a whole might become a *repository of anthropocenic signs*, how the earth will itself, in the future, display traces and remnants of a lost world that will retrospectively be identified as that of the Anthropocene.

Such an understanding of Chernobyl fits into the kinds of semiotic interpretations of the Anthropocene that I have analysed in previous chapters. While such a reading can be evocative and thought-provoking, as indeed O'Connell's musings on Chernobyl are, it remains very much governed by a specular logic that reflects and reproduces the present through the mirror of the future. In its self-reflexivity, such a reading risks glossing over the very real, and the very *living*, material realities out of which a place like Chernobyl is composed, realities that are not some mere trace or remnant of the past but that survive and continue to live and live on in the present, affecting countless human and non-human lives and inscribing themselves in the discursive and material practices that make up these realities. This is not some mere semiotic trace that lies inert, waiting to be read and given meaning. Chernobyl *survives* and *lives on* through the material, biological, ecological, social and economic inscriptions of its radioactivity. A materialist reading of Chernobyl is one that is attentive to these entangled inscriptions and the effects of their continued intra-active survivance.

The notion of mutation that Masco develops in his analysis of the Manhattan Project has allowed us to see how the decay of a radioactive isotope is entangled in the biological mutations that take place within the cells and the bodies of organisms, as well as in wider material, biological and ecological contexts. These changes are the product of intra-actions within and between various phenomena, and they themselves give rise to many other cascading transformations that can in turn impact the continued survivance of radioactive materials. An example from Chernobyl can help illustrate this. Radiation can cause changes to bacteria, fungi and invertebrates in ways that disrupt microbial activities in the soil and interrupt the decay and decomposition of organic materials. Studies of forest sites within or close to the Chernobyl Exclusion Zone show evidence of such reduced decomposition, leading to a build-up of leaf litter and dead wood on the forest floor.[51] This affects the growth of plants and trees as well as animal species that rely on such plants and trees for food and habitat. But it can also indirectly affect the distribution and redistribution of radionuclides themselves within this environment. Together with changes in rainfall patterns and other climatic phenomena, the build-up of dead wood and leaves has been linked to an increased risk of forest fire, which raises the prospect of the possible remobilisation and redistribution of radioactive fallout.[52] Regular wildfires in the Chernobyl Exclusion Zone burn through these contaminated materials, resulting in a renewed spread of contaminated smoke and ash which can transport the always-surviving, always-decaying radionuclides from the Exclusion Zone into new environments. This creates fresh cycles of cascading intra-active mutations and transformations that entangle other forms of living and non-living matter in the ongoing survivance of these radioactive isotopes.

These cascading intra-active transformations are as social, political, economic and discursive as they are biological and chemical. The development of nuclear science is intimately tied up with the history of the Second World War and the complex political, social, economic, military and technoscientific discourses and practices that culminated in the development of Cold War nuclear technologies.[53] One can think here of all the complex material, biological and discursive entanglements that led to the development of nuclear reactors and power plants like that set up in Chernobyl in 1977, all the different factors that contributed to the running of these plants and the very specific set of circumstances that led to the accident on April 26, 1986. But we can also think of the way that the *effects* of this accident have been compounded by political, scientific, social, economic and cultural discourses and practices. In her analysis of the Chernobyl disaster, Kate Brown shows in great detail how knowledge and information about the disaster itself, as well as on the effects of nuclear contamination and radiation more generally, was produced, controlled and withheld in the immediate aftermath of the accident and in the years since in ways that have greatly impacted the situation on the ground.[54] Brown also details how specific efforts to manage and contain the spread of the disaster—such as by redirecting rainclouds away from

Russian cities[55]—influenced the path of radioactive fallout, and she outlines how contaminated radionuclides were spread far beyond the limits of the Exclusion Zone through the distribution and selling of contaminated food-stuff and other agricultural products.[56] Human political, scientific, economic, social and cultural discourses and practices are all intimately entangled in the intra-active material and biological mutations outlined above in ways that exemplify how the material survivance I am tracking here cuts across differ-ent, but always entangled, material-biological-discursive realities.

Masco describes his concept of mutation as having 'bio-social' implica-tions,[57] and he notes that these can blur the distinction between nature and culture, allowing us to speak of 'nature-culture' as entangled phenomena.[58] None of these phenomena ever exist independently of one another because the material, biological and discursive entanglements I have outlined here are always co-constitutive of one another. These entities, practices and processes emerge out of one another, and they survive *in, as* and *because* of these intra-actions. Barad makes a similar point when she traces the multiple and complex discursive and material entanglements that link 'mushrooms' to 'mushroom clouds.' Barad notes that from 'radiotrophic mushrooms thriving in nuclear contaminated areas' and 'wildlife thriving around the reactors in Chernobyl,' to the 'racism, internment camps, war, militarism, imperialism, fascism, capitalism, [and] industrial expansion' that have been part and parcel of the global military and technoscientific nuclear complex for the past eighty years or so, 'all these material-discursive phenomena are constituted through each other, each in specifically entangled ways.'[59] The Anthropocene and the survivance of radionuclides in the strata of the earth are inscribed out of these entangled realities, and they continue to live such entangled lives. The survivance of these radioactive isotopes, of human and non-human forms of life, of ecological environments and of discursive practices is always a survivance *in* and *with* diverse phenomena, one that is marked by the intra-active inscriptions of these different entities and envi-ronments in one another.

When a nuclear bomb or, for that matter, a nuclear reactor explodes, Barad explains, 'each radioactive bit of matter is an imploded diffraction pattern of spacetimemattering, a mushrooming of specific entangled pos-sible histories.'[60] The survivance of each radioactive isotope consists of its continued intersection and intra-action with other material, biological and discursive forms of survivance within different environments and contexts, and this is what constitutes its material inscription in the strata of the earth. I have argued throughout the preceding chapters that if we are to continue to think of radioactive isotopes in soil and rock sediments as inscriptions of the

Anthropocene, then we must rethink our very understanding of what constitutes such an inscription. The anthropocenic trace should not be thought of as some dead inert mark that simply points back to what once was—an absolute signature that refers back to one specific place, one specific time and one specific signatory,[61] functioning as indelible proof of the existence of human beings and their activities upon this earth. The survivance of these isotopes is indeed always intimately entangled with human discursive, biological and material practices—most obviously in the complex engineering processes that were involved in the production of nuclear weapons and nuclear reactors, the events that led to the radioactive fallout from nuclear explosions, and the ongoing activities that continue to influence how radioactive materials behave within these environments. But the behaviour of these isotopes can never simply be limited to such human 'influences,' and these very 'influences' are themselves never simply the product of some singular human action or intent. 'Reading' and 'writing' are not unilateral processes, and, as I have shown, they can extend far beyond the limits of human activity. These radioactive traces constitute ongoing inscriptions that are and will remain active, still always mutating, still interacting and intra-acting with and within their environments. It is *this* that will continue to persist and survive in the strata of the earth hundreds, thousands or even millions of years from now. For as long as they last, these radionuclides will continue to intra-act in entangled cascading mutations of decomposition and recomposition, always *surviving* and *inscribing* themselves in and with their environments—even if the only environment that is eventually left is that of the isotopes themselves and everything else that they have irradiated.

Notes

1. "Results of Binding Vote by AWG," Anthropocene Working Group, May 21, 2019, http://quaternary.stratigraphy.org/working-groups/anthropocene/. As Colin Waters and his colleagues explain, radiation from nuclear tests and bombings between 1945, when the first Trinity test was held, and 1963, when the Partial Nuclear Test Ban Treaty came into effect, 'created an extremely distinctive radiogenic signature—a unique pattern of radioactive isotopes captured in the layers of the planet's marine and lake sediments, rock, and glacial ice that can serve as a clear, easily detected bookmark for the start of a new chapter in our planet's history' (Colin N. Waters et al., "Can Nuclear Weapons Fallout Mark the Beginning of the Anthropocene Epoch?" *Bulletin of the Atomic Scientists* 71, no. 3 (November 2015): 47). Jan Zalasiewicz is more specific in his predications, placing his bets on 'a big bomb spike somewhere between 1952 and 1954 that is quite distinct and unmistakable' (Jan Zalasiewicz cited in Meera Subramanian, "Humans versus Earth: The Quest to De-

fine the Anthropocene," *Nature*, August 6, 2019, https://www.nature.com/articles/ d41586-019-02381-2).

2. As the AWG explains, there are various phenomena associated with the Anthropocene, including an increase in rock erosion and sedimentation as a result of urbanisation and agriculture; changes to the quantities of carbon and other chemical elements, metals and compounds in the earth and in the atmosphere; rising global temperatures and sea levels; ocean acidification; habitat loss; and the existence of manmade materials, such as concrete and plastic. These phenomena, the group notes, 'are being reflected in a distinctive body of geological strata now accumulating' on the earth, but it is the nuclear 'signature' that is most likely to present a long-lasting, clearly distinguishable and consistent trace in the stratigraphic record ("Results of Binding Vote by AWG").

3. Elizabeth Kolbert, *The Sixth Extinction: An Unnatural History* (London: Bloomsbury, 2014), 105.

4. Tobias Menely and Jesse Oak Taylor, eds., *Anthropocene Reading: Literary History in Geologic Times* (University Park: Pennsylvania State University Press, 2017), 8.

5. Certain nuclear isotopes have extremely short half-lives and decay in a matter of milliseconds or less. Others, however, persist for far longer, for lengths of time that can be unimaginable to the human mind. Plutonium-239, for instance, has a half-life of around twenty-four thousand years.

6. Kate Brown, "Marie Curie's Fingerprint: Nuclear Spelunking in the Chernobyl Zone," in *Arts of Living on a Damaged Planet*, ed. Anna Tsing, Heather Swanson, Elaine Gan, and Nils Bubandt (Minneapolis: University of Minnesota Press, 2017), G41.

7. Brown, "Marie Curie," G37.

8. Susan Schuppli, "Radical Contact Prints," in *Camera Atomica*, ed. John O'Brian (London: Black Dog, 2014), 286; emphasis added.

9. Schuppli, "Radical Contact Prints," 279, 286.

10. Schuppli, "Radical Contact Prints," 280–81.

11. Schuppli, "Radical Contact Prints," 287.

12. Brown, "Marie Curie," G37.

13. Schuppli, "Radical Contact Prints," 286.

14. Brown, "Marie Curie," G36–37.

15. Joseph Masco, *The Nuclear Borderlands: The Manhattan Project in Post–Cold War New Mexico* (Princeton, NJ: Princeton University Press, 2006), 30.

16. Masco, *Nuclear Borderlands*, 28.

17. Schuppli, "Radical Contact Prints," 286.

18. Brown, "Marie Curie," G41.

19. Karen Barad, "Troubling Time/s and Ecologies of Nothingness: Re-turning, Re-membering, and Facing the Incalculable," *New Formations: A Journal of Culture/ Theory/Politics* 92 (2018): 74, https://doi.org/10.3898/NEWF:92.05.2017.

20. See my previous discussion of Derrida's "Des Tours de Babel" and Benjamin's "Task of the Translator" in Chapter 3 for more on the spectrality of this 'living on' through otherness.

21. I borrow this term from Derrida, who in *Specters of Marx* distinguishes between the *ontological*, which is anchored in a logic of presence, and the *hauntological*, which questions the possibility of any such presence and recognises its irreducible spectrality (Jacques Derrida, *Specters of Marx: The State of the Debt, the Work of Mourning, and the New International*, trans. Peggy Kamuf (New York: Routledge, 1994), 9–10).

22. Masco, *Nuclear Borderlands*, 30.

23. Masco, *Nuclear Borderlands*, 31–32.

24. Masco, *Nuclear Borderlands*, 80.

25. Siegfried S. Hecker and Joseph C. Martz, "Aging of Plutonium and Its Alloys," *Los Alamos Science* 26 (2000): 238.

26. Masco, *Nuclear Borderlands*, 80.

27. Significantly, though, the terms used to describe radioactive decay are strikingly similar to those used by biologists when referring to cell division. Nuclear physicists and chemists refer to *parent nuclides* and *daughter nuclides*, recalling the way that biologists also speak of a *parent* cell and the *daughter* cells that are formed through the process of mitosis.

28. Martin Hägglund links 'the logic of survival' to 'the general co-implication of persistence and destruction' of inanimate materials, and he uses the decay and survival of radioactive isotopes as an example of this. Hägglund argues that 'if something survives it is never present in itself; it is already marked by the destruction of a past that is no longer while persisting for a future that is not yet' (Martin Hägglund, "Radical Atheist Materialism: A Critique of Meillassoux," in *The Speculative Turn: Continental Materialism and Realism*, ed. Levi Bryant, Nick Srnicek, and Graham Harman (Melbourne: re.press, 2011), 122–23). Here I broaden the condition of spectrality that is implicit in this logic of survival *beyond* this relationship between past and future in order to consider the entanglement of material, biological or discursive entities in and with one another.

29. Hecker and Martz, "Aging of Plutonium," 140–43.

30. For more on this see the Natural and Accelerated Bioremediation Research Program, *Bioremediation of Metals and Radionuclides: What It Is and How It Works*, 2nd ed. (Lawrence Berkeley National Laboratory: U.S. Department of Energy, 2003), 23; and Abdelhamid H. Elgazzar and Nafisa Kazem, "Biological Effects of Ionizing Radiation," in *The Pathophysiologic Basis of Nuclear Medicine*, ed. Abdelhamid H. Elgazzar (New York: Springer, 2015), 716–17.

31. For more on this see Benedikta Luksiene et al., "Effect of Microorganisms on the Plutonium Oxidation States," *Applied Radiation and Isotopes* 70, no. 3 (March 2012): 442–49, https://doi.org/10.1016/j.apradiso.2011.11.016.

32. G. R. Choppin and A. Morgenstern, "Distribution and Movement of Environmental Plutonium," in *Plutonium in the Environment: Proceedings of the Second International Symposium November 9–12, 1999, Osaka, Japan*, ed. A. Kudo (Oxford:

Elsevier, 2000), 92; Wolfgang Rund, "The Chemical Interactions of Actinides in the Environment," *Los Alamos Science* 26 (2000): 393; Baikuntha P. Aryal et al., "Plutonium Uptake and Distribution in Mammalian Cells: Molecular vs. Polymeric Plutonium," *International Journal of Radiation Biology* 87, no. 10 (2011): 1023–32, https://doi.org/10.3109/09553002.2011.584941; and *Bioremediation of Metals and Radionuclides*, 10–14, 49–50.

33. Many of these processes form the basis of bioremediation projects which use the intra-actions between microorganisms and radionuclides in an attempt to manage the decay of these materials. For more on this see *Bioremediation of Metals and Radionuclides*.

34. Michael Peterson, "Responsibility and the Non(bio)degradable," in *Eco-Deconstruction: Derrida and Environmental Philosophy*, ed. Matthias Fritsch, Philippe Lynes, and David Wood (New York: Fordham University Press, 2018), 255.

35. It is worth recalling here Karen Barad's description of intra-action as '*the mutual constitution of entangled agencies*.' Barad distinguishes this from 'the usual "interaction," which assumes that there are separate individual agencies that precede their interaction' (Karen Barad, *Meeting the Universe Halfway: Quantum Physics and the Entanglement of Matter and Meaning* (Durham, NC: Duke University Press, 2007), 33).

36. Masco, *Nuclear Borderlands*, 30.

37. Masco describes the nuclear bomb as 'a multigenerational, national-cultural, economic, and environmental mutation' that has itself created 'a fundamental mutation in American life' (Masco, *Nuclear Borderlands*, 38–39). Masco develops 'a theory of mutation' that allows him to explore 'debates about the global effects of the bomb,' examine 'the traumatic effects of blast and radiation on living beings produced during the Cold War U.S. nuclear testing program,' interrogate 'how specific radioactive environments have been officially rescripted in the post–Cold War period as ecological "improvements"' and consider 'how the idea of the "nuclear worker" now links humans and wildlife within a shared genetic experiment in northern New Mexico [. . .] producing a highly ambiguous and charged social space' (Masco, *Nuclear Borderlands*, 293).

38. Genetic mutation was described in Chapter 2 as a manifestation of difference and otherness that inscribes itself in the processes of DNA replication and cellular reproduction by which biological life renews itself and survives. These manifestations of difference have traditionally been thought of as random errors. Indeed, François Jacob describes them as 'faults of production' or 'accidents' in the copying mechanism of the cell, errors that occur 'blindly' like typographic mistakes in the transcription of a text (François Jacob, *The Logic of Life: A History of Heredity*, trans. Betty E. Spillmann (New York: Pantheon Books, 1973), 288–89). But more recent research has shown that such mutations do not simply arise randomly; they can also be the result of external *epigenetic* factors that influence the genetic makeup of an organism. One such factor is nuclear radiation. As I show in what follows, mutations arising from epigenetic factors can influence the organism itself, and they can also be carried into the germ line, where they may be passed down to offspring.

39. George L. Voelz, "Plutonium and Health: How Great Is the Risk?" *Los Alamos Science* 26 (2000): 77.

40. Amanda L. Ogilvy-Stuart and Stephen M. Shalet, "Effect of Radiation on the Human Reproductive System," *Environmental Health Perspectives Supplements* 101, no. 2 (July 1993): 109–16, https://doi.org/10.2307/3431383.

41. Marie-Andree Esnault, Florence Legue, and Christian Chenal, "Ionizing Radiation: Advances in Plant Response," *Environmental and Experimental Botany* 68, no. 3 (May 2010): 234–35, https://doi.org/10.1016/j.envexpbot.2010.01.007. The mutations that take place within a cell as a result of radiation exposure are themselves already entangled in many other diverse biological, ecological and environmental phenomena that can affect how these changes manifest themselves in an organism and, more broadly, within wider populations and species. Studies of the impact of radioactive fallout on pine trees around Chernobyl, for instance, show that the size and shape of a tree affects its response to radiation, as do certain climatic and environmental factors, such as temperature and soil conditions (Timothy Mousseau et al., "Tree Rings Reveal Extent of Exposure to Ionizing Radiation in Scots Pine Pinus Sylvestris," *Trees* 27, no. 5 (June 2013): 1443–53, https://doi.org/10.1007/s00468-013-0891-z). Relationships between species and the competition for resources can also determine an organism's genetic and physical response to radiation, increasing or decreasing its radio-sensitivity, and these responses can themselves in turn also lead to complex secondary changes that can have wider repercussions on ecosystems as a whole (Stanislav A. Geras'kin, "Ecological Effects of Exposure to Enhanced Levels of Ionizing Radiation," *Journal of Environmental Radioactivity* 162–63 (October 2016): 347–48).

42. Geras'kin, "Ecological Effects," 348.

43. Anders Pape Møller and Timothy A. Mousseau, "Assessing Effects of Radiation on Abundance of Mammals and Predator-Prey Interactions in Chernobyl Using Tracks in the Snow," *Ecological Indicators* 26 (March 2013): 112–16, https://doi.org/10.1016/j.ecolind.2012.10.025.

44. Anders Pape Møller, Florian Barnier, and Timothy A. Mousseau, "Ecosystems Effects 25 Years After Chernobyl: Pollinators, Fruit Set and Recruitment," *Oecologia* 170, no. 4 (June 2012): 1155–65, https://doi.org/10.1007/s00442-012-2374-0.

45. Geras'kin, "Ecological Effects," 349.

46. Masco, *Nuclear Borderlands*, 301.

47. Masco, *Nuclear Borderlands*, 293–302.

48. As Masco describes them, these can include 'new adaptation[s] to the environment' that provide organisms with an evolutionary advantage, 'injur[ies] such as cancer or deformity,' or 'genetic noise [. . .] that neither improve[s] nor injure[s] the organism but can still affect future generations' (Masco, *Nuclear Borderlands*, 301).

49. Alan Weisman, *The World Without Us* (London: Virgin Books, 2007), 217.

50. Mark O'Connell, *Notes from an Apocalypse: A Personal Journey to the End of the World and Back* (London: Granta, 2020), 213, 183.

51. Anders Pape Møller and Timothy A. Mousseau, "Reduced Colonization by Soil Invertebrates to Irradiated Decomposing Wood in Chernobyl," *The Science of the Total Environment* 645 (July 2018): 778, https://doi.org/773–79.10.1016/j.scitotenv.2018.07.195; Timothy Mousseau et al., "Highly Reduced Mass Loss Rates and Increased Litter Layer in Radioactively Contaminated Areas," *Oecologia* 175, no. 1 (March 2014): 429–37, https://doi.org/10.1007/s00442-014-2908-8.

52. Nikolaos Evangeliou et al., "Wildfires in Chernobyl-Contaminated Forests and Risks to the Population and the Environment: A New Nuclear Disaster About to Happen?" *Environment International* 73 (December 2014): 346–58, https://doi.org/10.1016/j.envint.2014.08.012; Mousseau et al. "Highly Reduced," 436.

53. The development of such nuclear technologies is linked to the colonisation and destruction of native lands (including, of course, through the testing of nuclear weaponry), the uprooting of indigenous communities, the exploitation of low-income workers in American and Soviet 'plutonium cities' and many other forms of violence and exploitation (for more on this see Masco, *Nuclear Borderlands*, and Kate Brown, *Plutopia: Nuclear Families, Atomic Cities, and the Great Soviet and American Plutonium Disasters* (Oxford: Oxford University Press, 2013)).

54. As Brown notes, the official death toll from the Chernobyl disaster is registered as fifty-four deaths despite extensive evidence of tens and even hundreds of thousands of deaths (Kate Brown, *Manual for Survival: A Chernobyl Guide to the Future* (London: Penguin, 2020), 3). Brown argues that till this day 'the public is left at a scientific stalemate' over the true extent of the human and ecological disaster. This lack of knowledge, or, at least, the unwillingness to reveal the true effects of such disasters, continues to impact the way that new incidents are dealt with. Brown notes that 'after the Fukushima accident in 2011, scientists told the public they had no certain knowledge of the effects of low-dose exposures of radiation to human beings. They asked citizens for patience, for ten to twenty years, while they studied this new catastrophe, as if it were the first' (Brown, *Manual*, 3).

55. Brown, *Manual*, 40–45.

56. 'The Zone of Alienation,' Brown explains, 'was just a circle drawn on a map. It didn't stop radiation from transgressing its borders' (Brown, *Manual*, 86).

57. Masco, *Nuclear Borderlands*, 31.

58. Masco, *Nuclear Borderlands*, 301.

59. Karen Barad, "No Small Matter: Mushroom Clouds, Ecologies of Nothingness, and Strange Topologies of Spacetimemattering," in *Arts of Living*, Tsing, Swanson, Gan, and Bubandt, G116–17.

60. Barad, "No Small Matter," G116.

61. As Derrida explains, signatures mark the 'having-been' of a signer at a particular time and in a particular place (Jacques Derrida, "Signature Event Context," in *Limited Inc.*, trans. Samuel Weber and Jeffrey Mehlman (Evanston, IL: Northwestern University Press, 1988), 20); they constitute what Derrida refers to in "Biodegradables" as 'the singular mark of the event, of the date' (Jacques Derrida, "Biodegradables: Seven Diary Fragments," in *Signature Derrida*, trans. Peggy Kamuf, ed. Jay

Williams (Chicago: University of Chicago Press, 2013), 180). But for a signature to be legible, it must also be transposable into new contexts. As Derrida explains, 'in order to function, that is, to be readable, a signature must have a repeatable, iterable, imitable form; it must be able to be detached from the present and singular intention of its production' (Derrida, "Signature Event Context," 20).

~

Conclusion

Rewriting the Anthropocene

Many scientific and cultural discourses and practices of our time are structured by an anthropocentric and anthropocenic logic that works to affirm the continued value and significance of human beings upon the earth even in the face of their own potential demise. Indeed, as we have seen, the very notion of the Anthropocene functions as a specular device—or what Eileen Crist calls 'a Promethean self-portrait'[1]—that reflects the figure of the human back at itself through an imagined future anthropomorphic gaze that legitimises, validates and redeems the anthropocentric world of the present. The notion of the Anthropocene might appear to chastise human beings for the damage they have wrought upon the planet, but in recognising the supposed power that human beings now have upon the earth, it effectively also glorifies and deifies them. As Crist notes, the discourses of the Anthropocene present the human as 'an ingenious if unruly species, distinguishing itself from the background of merely-living life, rising so as to earn itself a separate name (anthropos meaning "man," and always implying "not-animal").'[2] Descriptions of the human as being 'on par with Nature's own tremendous forces' create an 'awed subtext' of 'human specialness' that confirms humankind's presumed exceptionality upon the earth and legitimises the narratives, discourses and practices that created the environmental and climate crises we now face.[3]

Through the perpetuating of its anthropocentric logic, the notion of the Anthropocene represents and continues to enact the many different forms of violence by which human beings have, over many centuries, exploited and commodified the earth. But the discourse of the Anthropocene and, indeed, the history of Western capitalist and industrialist expansion that it emerges out of, are not merely predicated on anthropocentric notions of human exceptionality that do violence to *non-human* forms of life and matter; they are also structured by a related racialised logic that values and acknowledges *certain forms of human life* over others. The positing of a singular '*anthropos*' as signatory of the Anthropocene and 'name-bearer'—or 'onomatophore'[4]—for the entire human species annuls the differences that exist amongst human beings, and it conceals the histories of violence by which many groups of people have been enslaved, exploited, slaughtered, oppressed and silenced in the creation of our so-called anthropocenic world. As Kathryn Yusoff and many others have argued, the construction of a 'monolithic' conception of the human 'erases the very racialized ruptures and geosocial rifts that brought this Anthropocenic world into being,'[5] and, through this very erasure, it continues to perpetuate this same violence. As an epoch and as a concept, the Anthropocene is constructed on the back of this double violence: the violence by which this world was brought into being and the violence by which this history continues to be erased in the construction and conceptualisation of a universalised *anthropos*.

The notion of a singular *anthropos* effaces difference, it erases marks of violence and evades responsibility—it enacts what Bonneuil and Fressoz describe as a 'totalisation of the entirety of human actions into a single "human activity",' positing 'an abstract humanity uniformly involved—and, it implies, uniformly to blame'—for the violence of the Anthropocene.[6] There is no singular 'I' or 'we' that could encompass all human beings upon the earth, and it is clear that not all human beings have played the same role in the creation of the heavily industrialised, capitalist world of the present. For such violence to be addressed, Bonneuil and Fressoz argue, invocations of a single human signatory that is representative of all of humankind should be rejected in favour of a different and 'differentiated' perspective that takes into account the vast economic, political, cultural, biological and geographic stratifications of power that many human beings have been subjected to. This challenge must be taken up, they explain, 'not just for the sake of historical truth, or to assess the responsibilities of the past, but also to pursue future policies that are more effective and more just.'[7] But, as Stacy Alaimo argues, any true engagement with the 'differentiality' of human beings also requires a 'shift from the sense of humans as an abstract force that acts but is not acted on to a *trans-corporeal* conception of the human as that which is always generated through and entangled in differing scales and sorts of biological, technological, economic, social, political, and other systems.'[8]

What must be rethought is not merely the question of *who* is responsible for the Anthropocene but the very way that this question is posed in the first place. A differentiated understanding of the Anthropocene requires that 'the human' cease to be thought of as 'a bounded being endowed with unilateral agency'[9] and is instead recognised as being intimately entangled in the many material and biological realities that are said to constitute its environment. What must be challenged is the very idea of the human itself as an independent entity that can serve as the ultimate referent or signatory of the anthropocenic trace, through an understanding of 'the extent to which human agencies are entangled with those of nonhuman creatures and inhuman substances and systems.'[10] As Alaimo notes, what we call 'the human' is always already entangled in 'nonhuman agencies and trajectories' in 'a multitude of intersecting biological and chemical, as well as geological, transformations, which intermesh human and natural histories.'[11]

Such an emphasis on the entangled, material nature of human existence underlies the use of a number of alternative terms for the Anthropocene—alternative '-cenes' that draw attention to the complex political, economic, social, cultural, biological, material and geological assemblages and networks of which human beings are always a part. The terms 'Capitalocene' and 'Plantationocene,'[12] for instance, point to the capitalist, industrialist and colonial underpinnings of the Anthropocene epoch and show how human actions are always entangled with other biological, geological and material phenomena in complex constellations of power, violence and oppression. Meanwhile, Donna Haraway's proposed term, 'Chthulucene,' invites even further consideration of how 'the effects of bioculturally, biotechnically, biopolitically, historically situated people' are always 'relative to, and combined with, the effects of other species assemblages and other biotic/abiotic forces.'[13] For Haraway, the Anthropocene cannot and should not be considered in solely human terms because human beings and their actions are always already part of much wider material, geological and biological entanglements. A productive engagement with the notion of the Anthropocene is thus one that recognises 'myriad temporalities and spatialities and myriad intra-active entities-in-assemblages—including the more-than-human, other-than-human, inhuman, and human-as-humus.'[14]

It is within the space opened up by such thought that my own understanding of the Anthropocene is situated. In my critique of the anthropocenic logic of future-retro-vision and my alterative reading of the textuality of the anthropocenic trace, I reject the idea of a single universalised *anthropos* acting as a signatory and name-bearer of the age, but, more importantly, I also problematise the assumption that the Anthropocene should be read *referentially* through a semiotic paradigm that remains, in essence, wholly human. From the perspective opened up by my critique, the so-called signature or trace of the Anthropocene in the strata of the earth appears less as a representational sign that points to a specific human referent and point of origin and more as an enactment of ongoing human and non-human, animate and inanimate entanglement that cuts across different material, biological and discursive boundaries. Rather than read the Anthropocene as a spectral human past that is written into the strata of the earth in a way that will continue to have meaning in the future, I have argued that we should consider how the very acts of anthropocenic reading and writing that we presume to be solely human can be recognised as being entangled in many other forms of material textuality that have *significance* even though they may not *signify* anything at all.

Acknowledging this entanglement does not mean that human beings can be absolved of any wrongdoing or that questions of culpability can be set aside in the name of some indistinct and unaccountable non-human agency. Quite the opposite, in fact. As Alaimo asserts, it is only through an understanding of entanglement that the full extent and effect of anthropocenic violence can be recognised and its acts of erasure revealed.[15] An understanding of entanglement can elucidate the complex ways in which different forms of violence are constructed (such as through the discursive, academic, political and material forms of bio- and geo-power that Yusoff calls 'White Geology'[16]), and it can open up ways of tracing the effects of this violence across communities, species and environments (as demonstrated by Karen Barad's writings on the effects of nuclear radiation,[17] Stacy Alaimo's trans-corporeal analyses of 'bodily natures,'[18] and the explorations of the 'haunted landscapes of the Anthropocene' undertaken by contributors to the volume *Arts of Living on a Damaged Planet*[19]). Such thinking invites alternative understandings of the Anthropocene that resist the structures of power, exploitation, abuse and oppression out of which the world of the present has been created, and it can provide us with the language we need to speak, write and live this resistance.

It is the effacement of difference, of otherness, of non-white, non-Western, non-imperialist, non-patriarchal, non-capitalist, non-human and non-binary lives and ways of life that has fuelled the Anthropocene, and it is this same effacement that continues to feed its universalising discourses. This effacement is governed by an anthropocentric and racialised logic that valorises *life, human life* and, more specifically, *certain kinds of human life* over any and every other form of human or non-human biological and material existence. As Yusoff argues, the racialised 'materiality' and 'grammar' of the

Anthropocene[20]—the material-discursive systems of geo- and bio-power by which this epoch has been brought into existence and through which it continues to be conceptualised—operate through the maintaining of a distinct boundary between life and matter, the human and the non-human and the animate and the inanimate that paradoxically works to *dehumanise, objectify* and *commodify* groups of human beings (together with non-human organisms and a supposedly inanimate earth) and to legitimate the violence and injustices enacted against them. This is a manifestation of what Elizabeth Povinelli calls 'geontopower,' described as 'a set of discourse, affects, and tactics used in late liberalism to maintain or shape the coming relationship of the distinction between Life and Nonlife.'[21] Through these divisions, the supposedly inert, inhuman and inanimate is devalued and debased, groups of human beings are themselves relegated to this devalued category and treated as material resources[22] and other ways of viewing and understanding the relationship between life and non-life are also annulled.[23]

One way of challenging these discourses and the violences that they enact is by rigorously interrogating these oppositions and boundaries and developing ways of understanding the relationships between human and non-human forms of life and matter that do not reduce *difference* (in all of its complex and entangled different and differential manifestations) to some *singular distinction*. This is, to a large extent, a challenge of language. Yusoff notes that what must be undone are the 'grammars' of geology and the 'language of materiality and its division between life and nonlife' in order to find 'mode[s] of writing' that are not inscribed in, and do not themselves continue to inscribe, such violence.[24] What is required is a fundamental transformation in the way that we think, speak and write about human, non-human, biological and material existence—but also, at the same time, a radical shift in the way that we think about *language* itself. If, as I have argued in this volume, human discursive structures are diffractively entangled in other forms of biological and material textuality, then the ways in which we think and speak about the world *intra-actively shape* the world while also being *shaped* by it. If language is diffractively and differentially entangled in the many material phenomena that constitute earthly reality, then it can also materially and diffractively make a difference on this earth.

We saw in the introduction to this volume how in his writings on the apocalypse Günther Anders laments our inability to speak and think about the end of the world—to put into words the unimaginable 'nothingness' that the world will be plunged into following the possible destruction and ultimate extinction of the human species. As we have seen, these laments are echoed in more recent commentaries on the Anthropocene which call for a reckoning for our species, urging us to confront the notion of apocalypse and the possibility of future species extinction in the hopes that we might be jolted out of our collective apathy and inertia. But, as I have argued throughout this volume, what is needed is not simply a way of thinking and representing the possible absence of human beings upon this planet—a language and a form of thought that would challenge us to imagine the end of the world and the end of human beings upon it while paradoxically also continuing to only grant value and significance to *human* forms of presence and absence. What are required are modes of thinking, speaking and writing that disrupt the very concept of *presence* itself—and the notions of individuality and autonomy that underlie it—and that recognise how language, thought, representation, value and significance are only ever possible as a result of the complex material, biological and discursive entanglements of which human beings are just one part.

In her materialist rereadings of Derrida and Saussure, Vicki Kirby contends that 'the archive of the world, or more accurately, an archive of world-ing, [. . .] present[s] itself in every word, underwriting the flesh of every name—every calculation.'[25] '[L]anguage, representation, modeling,' Kirby tells us, are not particular to human uses of language; they are also 'what the world does in its ongoing manufacture.'[26] If our own uses of language are entangled in the more general textuality of different material and biological realities, then language does not merely *reflect* or *represent* reality; it *enacts*, *performs* and very intimately *participates* in it. The materialist engagements with Derridean thought that I have developed throughout this volume have sought to explore and exemplify this, demonstrating through the use of specific diffractive paradigms how the language that we use to think, to speak and to write about material entanglement can *itself* also enact such entanglement. This should serve to remind us that the ways in which we speak, write and think about the world *actually matter* and that our collective *rereadings* of the Anthropocene can also constitute a potential *rewriting* of this discursive and material phenomenon. Such a rewriting can change our conceptualisations of what the Anthropocene *means*, but, more importantly, it can perhaps also change what it is that the Anthropocene actually turns out to *be*.

Notes

1. Eileen Crist, "On the Poverty of Our Nomenclature," in *Anthropocene or Capitalocene? Nature, History, and the Crisis of Capitalism*, ed. Jason W. Moore (Oakland, CA: PM Press, 2016), 16.
2. Crist, "On the Poverty," 16.

3. Crist, "On the Poverty," 16–17.

4. Bronislaw Szerszynski, "The End of the End of Nature: The Anthropocene and the Fate of the Human," *The Oxford Literary Review* 34, no. 2 (December 2012): 173, https://doi.org/10.3366/olr.2012.0040 169.

5. Kathryn Yusoff, *A Billion Black Anthropocenes or None* (Minneapolis: University of Minnesota Press, 2018), 57–58. As Yusoff notes, 'the passage to universalism in ecological or planetary terms' occurs 'without a redress of how that humanity was borne as an exclusionary construct, coterminous with the enslavement of some humans and the genocide of others' (Yusoff, *A Billion Black Anthropocenes*, 53).

6. Christophe Bonneuil and Jean-Baptiste Fressoz, *The Shock of the Anthropocene*, trans. David Fernbach (London: Verso, 2017), 65–66.

7. Bonneuil and Fressoz, *Shock of the Anthropocene*, 71.

8. Stacy Alaimo, "Your Shell on Acid: Material Immersion, Anthropocene Dissolves," in *Anthropocene Feminism*, ed. Richard A. Grusin (Minneapolis: University of Minnesota Press, 2017), 101; emphasis added.

9. Alaimo, "Your Shell on Acid," 89.

10. Alaimo, "Your Shell on Acid," 90.

11. Alaimo, "Your Shell on Acid," 92, 94.

12. For more on the use of these terms see the contributions to *Anthropocene or Capitalocene? Nature, History, and the Crisis of Capitalism*, ed. Jason W. Moore (Oakland, CA: PM Press, 2016).

13. Donna Haraway, "Anthropocene, Capitalocene, Plantationocene, Chthulucene: Making Kin," *Environmental Humanities* 6, no. 1 (May 2015): 159, https://doi.org/10.1215/22011919-3615934.

14. Haraway, "Anthropocene, Capitalocene, Plantationocene, Chthulucene," 160.

15. Alaimo, "Your Shell on Acid," 101.

16. Yusoff, *A Billion Black Anthropocenes*.

17. See, for instance, "Troubling Time/s and Ecologies of Nothingness: Returning, Re-membering, and Facing the Incalculable," *New Formations: A Journal of Culture/Theory/Politics* 92 (2018): 56–86, https://doi.org/10.3898/NEWF:92.05.2017; and no Small Matter: Mushroom Clouds, Ecologies of Nothingness, and Strange Topologies of Spacetimemattering," in *Arts of Living on a Damaged Planet*, ed. Anna Tsing, Heather Swanson, Elaine Gan, and Nils Bubandt (Minneapolis: University of Minnesota Press, 2017), G103–20.

18. Stacy Alaimo, *Bodily Natures: Science, Environment, and the Material Self* (Bloomington: Indiana University Press, 2010).

19. This phrase is taken from the introduction to the section "Ghosts on a Damaged Planet" in the collection *Arts of Living on a Damaged Planet* (Elaine Gan, Anna Tsing, Heather Swanson, and Nils Bubandt, "Introduction: Haunted Landscapes of the Anthropocene," in *Arts of Living*, G1–14).

20. Yusoff, *A Billion Black Anthropocenes*, xiv.

21. Elizabeth A. Povinelli, *Geontologies: A Requiem to Late Capitalism* (Durham, NC: Duke University Press, 2016), 4.

22. Povinelli, *Geontologies*, 70–73.

23. Povinelli, *Geontologies*, 5.

24. Yusoff, *A Billion Black Anthropocenes*, xii, 9, 52.

25. Vicki Kirby, *Quantum Anthropologies: Life at Large* (Durham, NC: Duke University Press, 2011), 47.

26. Kirby, *Quantum Anthropologies*, 133.

~

Bibliography

Ackerman, Diane. *The Human Age: The World Shaped by Us*. New York: Norton, 2014.

Alaimo, Stacy. *Bodily Natures: Science, Environment, and the Material Self*. Bloomington: Indiana University Press, 2010.

Alaimo, Stacy. "Your Shell on Acid: Material Immersion, Anthropocene Dissolves." In *Anthropocene Feminism*, edited by Richard A. Grusin, 89–120. Minneapolis: University of Minnesota Press, 2017.

Alaimo, Stacy, and Susan Heckman, eds. *Material Feminisms*. Bloomington: Indiana University Press, 2008.

Alcor. "A Brief Scientific Introduction to Cryonics." https://www.alcor.org/library/a-brief-scientific-introduction-to-cryonics/.

"An Ecomodernist Manifesto." April 2015. http://www.ecomodernism.org/7.

Anders, Günther. "Commandments in the Atomic Age." In *Philosophy and Technology: Readings in the Philosophical Problems of Technology*, edited by Carl Mitcham and Robert Mackey, 130–35. New York: Free Press, 1972.

Anders, Günther. "Die beweinte Zukunft." In *Die atomare Drohung: Radikale Überlegungen zum atomaren Zeitalter*, 1–10. Munich: C. H. Beck, 2003.

Anders, Günther. "Language and End Time (Sections I, IV, and V of 'Sprache und Endzeit')," translated by Christopher John Müller. *Thesis Eleven* 153, no. 1 (August 2019): 134–40. https://doi.org/10.1177/0725513619864448.

Anders, Günther. "Reflections on the H Bomb." *Dissent* 3, no. 2 (Spring 1956): 146–55.

Anders, Günther. "Theses for the Atomic Age." *The Massachusetts Review* 3, no. 3 (Spring 1962): 493–505.

Anthropocene Working Group. "Results of /binding Vote by AWG." May 21, 2019. http://quaternary.stratigraphy.org/working-groups/anthropocene/.

Aryal, Baikuntha P., et al. "Plutonium Uptake and Distribution in Mammalian Cells: Molecular vs. Polymeric Plutonium." *International Journal of Radiation Biology* 87, no. 10 (October 2011): 1023–32. https://doi.org/10.3109/09553002.2011.584941.

Baker, Victor R. "Geosemiosis." *Geological Society of America Bulletin* 111, no. 5 (May 1999): 633–45. https://doi.org/10.1130/0016-7606(1999)111<0633:G>2.3.CO;2.

Barad, Karen. "After the End of the World: Entangled Nuclear Colonialisms, Matters of Force, and the Material Force of Justice." *Theory & Event* 22, no. 3 (July 2019): 524–50.

Barad, Karen. *Meeting the Universe Halfway: Quantum Physics and the Entanglement of Matter and Meaning*. Durham, NC: Duke University Press, 2007.

Barad, Karen. "No Small Matter: Mushroom Clouds, Ecologies of Nothingness, and Strange Topologies of Spacetimemattering." In *Arts of Living on a Damaged Planet*, edited by Anna Tsing, Heather Swanson, Elaine Gan, and Nils Bubandt, G103–20. Minneapolis: University of Minnesota Press, 2017.

Barad, Karen. "Quantum Entanglements and Hauntological Relations of Inheritance: Dis/continuities, SpaceTime Enfoldings, and Justice-to-Come." *Derrida Today* 3, no. 2 (November 2010): 240–68. https://doi.org/10.3366/E1754850010000813.

Barad, Karen. "Troubling Time/s and Ecologies of Nothingness: Re-turning, Remembering, and Facing the Incalculable." *New Formations: A Journal of Culture/Theory/Politics* 92 (2018): 56–86. https://doi.org/10.3898/NEWF:92.05.2017.

Basile, Jonathan. "Misreading Generalised Writing: From Foucault to Speculative Realism and New Materialism." *Oxford Literary Review* 40, no. 1 (July 2018): 20–37. https://doi.org/10.3366/olr.2018.0236.

Bastian, Michelle, and Thom van Dooren. "Editorial Preface: The New Immortals: Immortality and Infinitude in the Anthropocene." *Environmental Philosophy* 14, no. 1 (Spring 2017): 1–9. https://doi.org/10.5840/envirophil20171411.

Beck, Ulrich. *World at Risk*. Translated by Ciaran Cronin. Cambridge: Polity, 2009.

Benjamin, Walter. "The Task of the Translator." Translated by Harry Zohn. In *Walter Benjamin Selected Writings*, Vol. 1, edited by Marcus Bullock and Michael W. Jennings, 253–63. Cambridge, MA: Harvard University Press, 1996.

Benjamin, Walter. "The Translator's Task." Translated by Steven Rendall. *TTR: traduction, terminologie, rédaction* 10, no. 2 (1997): 151–65.

Bennett, Jane. *Vibrant Matter: A Political Ecology of Things*. Durham, NC: Duke University Press, 2010.

Boes, Tobias, and Kate Marshall. "Writing the Anthropocene: An Introduction." *Minnesota Review*, no. 83 (November 2014): 60–72.

Bonneuil, Christophe, and Jean-Baptiste Fressoz. *The Shock of the Anthropocene*. Translated by David Fernbach. London: Verso, 2017.

Borresen, Kelsey. "The Psychology Behind Why We Lose Track of Time in Quarantine." *HuffPost*, April 24, 2020. https://www.huffpost.com/entry/psychology-time -quarantine_l_5e9e2095c5b6b2e5b836de6d.

Brown, Kate. *Manual for Survival: A Chernobyl Guide to the Future*. London: Penguin, 2020.

Brown, Kate. "Marie Curie's Fingerprint: Nuclear Spelunking in the Chernobyl Zone." In *Arts of Living on a Damaged Planet*, edited by Anna Tsing, Heather Swanson, Elaine Gan, and Nils Bubandt, G33–50. Minneapolis: University of Minnesota Press, 2017.

Brown, Kate. *Plutopia: Nuclear Families, Atomic Cities, and the Great Soviet and American Plutonium Disasters*. Oxford: Oxford University Press, 2013.

Bunning, Jonny. "The Freezer Program: Value After Life." In *Cryopolitics: Frozen Life in a Melting World*, edited by Joanna Radin and Emma Kowal, 215–43. Cambridge, MA: MIT Press, 2017.

Burgess, Kaya. "Space Ark Will Save Man from a Dying Planet." *The Times*, April 28, 2014. thetimes.co.uk/article/space-ark-will-save-man-from-a-dying-planet -c0xh08vzsb2.

Butman, Jeremy. "Deconstructive Empiricism: Science and Metaphor in Derrida's Early Work." *Derrida Today* 12, no. 2 (November 2019): 115–29. https://doi.org/10.3366/drt.2019.0205.

Chakrabarty, Dipesh. "The Climate of History: Four Theses." *Critical Inquiry* 35, no. 2 (Winter 2009): 197–222. https://doi.org/10.1086/596640.

Cheah, Pheng. "Non-Dialectical Materialism." In *New Materialisms: Ontology, Agency, and Politics*, edited by Diana Coole and Samantha Frost, 70–91. Durham, NC: Duke University Press, 2010.

Chen, Mel Y. *Animacies: Biopolitics, Racial Mattering, and Queer Affect*. Durham, NC: Duke University Press, 2012.

Choppin, G. R., and A. Morgenstern. "Distribution and Movement of Environmental Plutonium." In *Plutonium in the Environment: Proceedings of the Second International Symposium November 9–12, 1999, Osaka, Japan*, edited by A. Kudo, 91–106. Oxford: Elsevier, 2000.

Chow, Denise. "Three Islands Disappeared in the Past Year. Is Climate Change to Blame?" *NBC News*, June 9, 2019. https://www.nbcnews.com/mach/science/three -islands-disappeared-past-year-climate-change-blame-ncna1015316.

Chrulew, Matthew. "Freezing the Ark: The Cryopolitics of Endangered Species Preservation." In *Cryopolitics: Frozen Life in a Melting World*, edited by Joanna Radin and Emma Kowal, 283–306. Cambridge, MA: MIT Press, 2017.

Cohen, Jeffrey Jerome. *Stone: An Ecology of the Inhuman*. Minneapolis: University of Minnesota Press, 2016.

Cohen, Jeffrey Jerome, and Lowell Duckert, eds. *Elemental Ecocriticism: Thinking with Earth, Air, Water, and Fire*. Minneapolis: University of Minnesota Press, 2015.

Cohen, Tom, Claire Colebrook, and J. Hillis Miller. *Twilight of the Anthropocene Idols*. London: Open Humanities Press, 2016.

Colebrook, Claire. *Death of the PostHuman: Essays on Extinction*, Vol. 1. Ann Arbor, MI: Open Humanities Press, 2015.

Coole, Diana, and Samantha Frost, eds. *New Materialisms: Ontology, Agency, and Politics*. Durham, NC: Duke University Press, 2010.

Cooper, Geoffrey M. *The Cell: A Molecular Approach*, 8th ed. Oxford: Oxford University Press, 2019.

Crist, Eileen. "On the Poverty of Our Nomenclature." In *Anthropocene or Capitalocene? Nature, History, and the Crisis of Capitalism*, edited by Jason W. Moore, 14–33. Oakland, CA: PM Press, 2016.

Crist, Eileen, and Helen Kopnina. "Unsettling Anthropocentrism." *Dialectical Anthropology* 38 (December 2014): 387–96. https://doi.org/10.1007/s10624-014-9362-1.

Crop Trust. "Svalbard Global Seed Vault." Accessed June 16, 2021. https://www.croptrust.org/our-work/svalbard-global-seed-vault/.

Crutzen, Paul J., and Eugene F. Stoermer. "The 'Anthropocene.'" *Global Change Newsletter*, no. 41 (May 2000): 17–18.

Danowski, Déborah, and Eduardo Viveiros de Castro. *The Ends of the World*. Translated by Rodrigo Guimaraes Nunes. Cambridge: Polity Press, 2016.

Darwin, Charles. *The Origin of Species*. London: Penguin, 1968.

Day, Michael. "Noah's Ark for Plants to Store World's Seeds." *The Telegraph*, January 28, 2008. https://www.telegraph.co.uk/news/earth/earthnews/3323301/Noahs-Ark-for-plants-to-store-worlds-seeds.html.

Deer, Jemma. "Quenched: Five Fires for Thinking Extinction." *The Oxford Literary Review* 41, no. 1 (July 2019): 1–17. https://doi.org/10.3366/olr.2019.0262.

Derrida, Jacques. *Archive Fever: A Freudian Impression*. Translated by Erin Prenowitz. Chicago: University of Chicago Press, 1996.

Derrida, Jacques. "Biodegradables: Seven Diary Fragments." Translated by Peggy Kamuf. In *Signature Derrida*, edited by Jay Williams, 152–219. Chicago: University of Chicago Press, 2013.

Derrida, Jacques. *Demeure: Fiction and Testimony*. Translated by Elizabeth Rottenberg. Stanford, CA: Stanford University Press, 2000.

Derrida, Jacques. "Des Tours de Babel." Translated by Joseph F. Graham. In *Difference in Translation*, edited by Joseph F. Graham, 165–207. Ithaca, NY: Cornell University Press, 1985.

Derrida, Jacques. "Différance." In *Margins of Philosophy*. Translated by Alan Bass. Brighton: Harvester Press, 1982.

Derrida, Jacques. *Learning to Live Finally: The Last Interview*. Translated by Pascale-Anne Brault and Michael Naas. Hoboken, NJ: Melville House, 2007.

Derrida, Jacques. *Life Death*. Translated by Pascale-Anne Brault and Michael Naas. Chicago: University of Chicago Press, 2020.

Derrida, Jacques. *Of Grammatology*. Translated by Gayatri Chakravorty Spivak (corrected ed.). Baltimore: Johns Hopkins University Press, 1998.

Derrida, Jacques. "Signature Event Context." Translated by Samuel Weber and Jeffrey Mehlman. In *Limited Inc*. Evanston, IL: Northwestern University Press, 1988.

Derrida, Jacques. *Specters of Marx: The State of the Debt, the Work of Mourning, and the New International.* Translated by Peggy Kamuf. New York: Routledge, 1994.

Derrida, Jacques. *The Beast and the Sovereign,* Vol. 2. Translated by Geoffrey Bennington. Chicago: University of Chicago Press, 2011.

Dolphijn, Rick, and Iris van der Tuin. *New Materialism: Interviews and Cartographies.* Ann Arbor, MI: Open Humanities Press, 2012.

Douglas, Collin. "A Storm Without Rain: Yemen, Water, Climate Change, and Conflict." The Center for Climate and Security, August 3, 2016. https://climat eandsecurity.org/2016/08/a-storm-without-rain-yemen-water-climate-change -and-conflict/.

Doyle, Richard. *Wetwares: Experiments in Postvital Living.* Minneapolis: University of Minnesota Press, 2003.

Dupuy, Jean-Pierre. *A Short Treatise on the Metaphysics of Tsunamis.* Translated by M. B. DeBevoise. East Lansing: Michigan State University Press, 2015.

Dupuy, Jean-Pierre. "The Precautionary Principle and Enlightened Doomsaying: Rational Choice Before the Apocalypse." *Occasion: Interdisciplinary Studies in the Humanities* 1, no. 1 (October 2009): 1–13.

Elgazzar, Abdelhamid H., and Nafisa Kazem. "Biological Effects of Ionizing Radiation." In *The Pathophysiologic Basis of Nuclear Medicine,* edited by Abdelhamid H. Elgazzar, 715–26. New York: Springer, 2015.

Ellis, Erle C. "Forget Mother Nature: This Is a World of Our Making." *New Scientist,* June 8, 2011. https://www.newscientist.com/article/mg21028165-700-forget -mother-nature-this-is-a-world-of-our-making/.

Ellis, Erle C. "Neither Good nor Bad." *New York Times,* May 23, 2011. https:// www.nytimes.com/roomfordebate/2011/05/19/the-age-of-anthropocene-should -we-worry/neither-good-nor-bad.

Ellis, Erle C. "Planet of No Return: Human Resilience on an Artificial Earth." *Breakthrough Journal,* no. 2 (Fall 2011). https://thebreakthrough.org/journal/issue-2/ the-planet-of-no-return.

Environmental Justice Foundation. "Climate Displacement in Bangladesh." Accessed June 15, 2021. https://ejfoundation.org/reports/climate-displacement-in -bangladesh.

Esnault, Marie-Andree, Florence Legue, and Christian Chenal. "Ionizing Radiation: Advances in Plant Response." *Environmental and Experimental Botany* 68, no. 3 (May 2010): 231–37. https://doi.org/10.1016/j.envexpbot.2010.01.007.

Evangeliou, Nikolaos, et al. "Wildfires in Chernobyl-Contaminated Forests and Risks to the Population and the Environment: A New Nuclear Disaster About to Happen?" *Environment International* 73 (December 2014): 346–58. https://doi .org/10.1016/j.envint.2014.08.012.

Farrier, David. *Footprints: In Search of Future Fossils.* New York: Farrar, Straus and Giroux, 2020.

Fritsch, Matthias, Philippe Lynes, and David Wood, eds. *Eco-Deconstruction: Derrida and Environmental Philosophy.* New York: Fordham University Press, 2018.

Frozen Zoo. San Diego Zoo Wildlife Alliance. https://science.sandiegozoo.org/re-sources/frozen-zoo%C2%AE.

Gabrys, Jennifer. "Plastic and the Work of the Biodegradable." In *Accumulation: The Material Politics of Plastic*, edited by Jennifer Gabrys, Gay Hawkins, and Mike Michael, 208–27. London: Routledge, 2013.

Gamble, Christopher N., Joshua S. Hanan, and Thomas Nail. "What Is New Materialism?" *Angelaki* 24, no. 6 (December 2019): 111–34. https://doi.org/10.1080/09 69725X.2019.1684704122.

Gan, Elaine, Anna Tsing, Heather Swanson, and Nils Bubandt. "Introduction: Haunted Landscapes of the Anthropocene." In *Arts of Living on a Damaged Planet*, edited by Anna Tsing, Heather Swanson, Elaine Gan, and Nils Bubandt, G1–14. Minneapolis: University of Minnesota Press, 2017.

Geras'kin, Stanislav A. "Ecological Effects of Exposure to Enhanced Levels of Ionizing Radiation." *Journal of Environmental Radioactivity* 162–163 (October 2016): 347–57.

Gould, Stephen J. "Glow, Big Glowworm." *Natural History* 95, no. 12 (1986): 10–16.

Greer, John Michael. "2016: Toward the Deep Future." The Dark Mountain Project, January 19, 2017. https://dark-mountain.net/2016-toward-the-deep-future/.

Hägglund, Martin. *Radical Atheism: Derrida and the Time of Life*. Stanford, CA: Stanford University Press, 2008.

Hägglund, Martin. "Radical Atheist Materialism: A Critique of Meillassoux." In *The Speculative Turn: Continental Materialism and Realism*, edited by Levi Bryant, Nick Srnicek, and Graham Harman, 114–29. Melbourne: re.press, 2011.

Hamilton, Clive. *Defiant Earth: The Fate of Humans in the Anthropocene*. London: Polity, 2017.

Haraway, Donna. "Anthropocene, Capitalocene, Plantationocene, Chthulucene: Making Kin." *Environmental Humanities* 6, no. 1 (May 2015): 159–65. https://doi .org/10.1215/22011919-3615934.

Haraway, Donna J. *Staying with the Trouble: Making Kin in the Chthulucene*. Durham, NC: Duke University Press, 2016.

Hecker, Siegfried S., and Joseph C. Martz. "Aging of Plutonium and Its Alloys." *Los Alamos Science* 26 (2000): 238–43.

Heise, Ursula K. *Imagining Extinction: The Cultural Meanings of Endangered Species*. Chicago: University of Chicago Press, 2016.

Heringman, Noah. "The Anthropocene Reads Buffon; or, Reading Like Geology." In *Anthropocene Reading: Literary History in Geologic Times*, edited by Tobias Menely and Jesse Oak Taylor, 59–77. University Park: Pennsylvania State University Press, 2017.

Höhler, Sabine. *Spaceship Earth in the Environmental Age, 1960–1990*. London: Routledge, 2015.

Horvat, Srećko. *After the Apocalypse*. Cambridge: Polity, 2021.

Ialenti, Vincent. *Deep Time Reckoning: How Future Thinking Can Help Earth Now*. Cambridge, MA: MIT Press, 2020.

Iovino, Serenella, and Serpil Oppermann. *Material Ecocriticism*. Bloomington: Indiana University Press, 2014.

Iveson, Richard. "Being Without Life: On the Trace of Organic Chauvinism with Derrida and DeLanda." In *Philosophy After Nature*, edited by Rosi Braidotti and Rick Dolphijn, 179–94. London: Rowman & Littlefield International, 2017.

Jacob, François. *The Logic of Life: A History of Heredity*. Translated by Betty E. Spillmann. New York: Pantheon Books, 1973.

Jamieson, Dale. "The Anthropocene; Love It or Leave It." In *The Routledge Companion to the Environmental Humanities*, edited by Ursula K. Heise, Jon Christensen, and Michelle Niemann, 13–20. London: Routledge, 2017.

Johnson, Christopher. *System and Writing in the Philosophy of Jacques Derrida*. Cambridge: Cambridge University Press, 1993.

Kaplan, E. Ann. *Climate Trauma: Foreseeing the Future in Dystopian Film and Fiction*. New Brunswick, NJ: Rutgers University Press, 2016.

Kay, Lily E. *Who Wrote the Book of Life?: A History of the Genetic Code*. Stanford, CA: Stanford University Press, 2000.

Kingsnorth, Paul, and Dougald Hine. "Uncivilisation: The Dark Mountain Manifesto." The Dark Mountain Project, 2009. https://dark-mountain.net/about/manifesto/.

Kirby, Vicki. "Foreword." In *What if Culture Was Nature All Along*, edited by Vicki Kirby, viii–xii. Edinburgh: Edinburgh University Press, 2017.

Kirby, Vicki. "Matter Out of Place: 'New Materialism' in Review." In *What if Culture Was Nature All Along*, edited by Vicki Kirby, 1–25. Edinburgh: Edinburgh University Press, 2017.

Kirby, Vicki. *Quantum Anthropologies: Life at Large*. Durham, NC: Duke University Press, 2011.

Kolbert, Elizabeth. *The Sixth Extinction: An Unnatural History*. London: Bloomsbury, 2014.

Latour, Bruno. "Agency at the Time of the Anthropocene." *New Literary History* 45, no. 1 (2014): 1–18. https://doi.org/10.1353/nlh.2014.0003.

Lewis, Simon L., and Mark A. Maslin. "Defining the Anthropocene." *Nature* 519, no. 7542 (March 2015): 171–80. https://doi.org/10.1038/nature14258.

Luksiene, Benedikta, et al. "Effect of Microorganisms on the Plutonium Oxidation States." *Applied Radiation and Isotopes* 70, no. 3 (March 2012): 442–49. https://doi.org/10.1016/j.apradiso.2011.11.016.

Lynes, Philippe. *Futures of Life Death on Earth: Derrida's General Ecology*. London: Rowman & Littlefield International, 2018.

MacCormack, Patricia. *The Ahuman Manifesto: Activism for the End of the Anthropocene*. London: Bloomsbury, 2020.

Madsen, Michael. *Into Eternity: A Film for the Future*. Lise Lense-Møller, 2010.

Marder, Michael. *Plant Thinking: A Philosophy of Vegetal Life*. New York: Columbia University Press, 2013.

Masco, Joseph. *The Nuclear Borderlands: The Manhattan Project in Post–Cold War New Mexico*. Princeton, NJ: Princeton University Press, 2006.

McCance, Dawne. *The Reproduction of Life Death: Derrida's La vie la mort*. New York: Fordham University Press, 2019.

Meillassoux, Quentin. *After Finitude: An Essay on the Necessity of Contingency*. Translated by Ray Brassier. London: Continuum, 2008.

Menely, Tobias, and Jesse Oak Taylor, eds. *Anthropocene Reading: Literary History in Geologic Times*. University Park: Pennsylvania State University Press, 2017.

Mitman, Gregg. "Hubris or Humility? Genealogies of the Anthropocene." In *Future Remains: A Cabinet of Curiosities for the Anthropocene*, edited by Gregg Mitman, Marco Armiero, and Robert S. Emmett, 59–68. Chicago: University of Chicago Press, 2018.

Møller, Anders Pape, and Timothy A. Mousseau. "Assessing Effects of Radiation on Abundance of Mammals and Predator-Prey Interactions in Chernobyl Using Tracks in the Snow." *Ecological Indicators* 26 (March 2013): 112–16. https://doi.org/10.1016/j.ecolind.2012.10.025.

Møller, Anders Pape, and Timothy A. Mousseau. "Reduced Colonization by Soil Invertebrates to Irradiated Decomposing Wood in Chernobyl." *The Science of the Total Environment* 645 (July 2018). https://doi.org/773–79.10.1016/j.scitotenv.2018.07.195.

Møller, Anders Pape, Florian Barnier, and Timothy A. Mousseau. "Ecosystems Effects 25 Years After Chernobyl: Pollinators, Fruit Set and Recruitment." *Oecologia* 170, no. 4 (June 2012): 1155–65. https://doi.org/10.1007/s00442-012-2374-0.

Moore, Jason W, ed. *Anthropocene or Capitalocene? Nature, History, and the Crisis of Capitalism*. Oakland, CA: PM Press, 2016.

Morgan, Benjamin. "Scale as Form: Thomas Hardy's Rocks and Stars." In *Anthropocene Reading: Literary History in Geologic Times*, edited by Tobias Menely and Jesse Oak Taylor, 132–49. University Park: Pennsylvania State University Press, 2017.

Morton, Timothy. "Ecology as Text, Text as Ecology." *The Oxford Literary Review* 32, no. 1 (July 2010): 1–17. https://doi.org/10.3366/E03051498100006112.

Morton, Timothy. *Hyperobjects: Philosophy and Ecology After the End of the World*. Minneapolis: University of Minnesota Press, 2013.

Mousseau, Timothy, et al. "Highly Reduced Mass Loss Rates and Increased Litter Layer in Radioactively Contaminated Areas." *Oecologia* 175, no. 1 (March 2014): 429–37. https://doi.org/10.1007/s00442-014-2908-8.

Mousseau, Timothy, et al. "Tree Rings Reveal Extent of Exposure to Ionizing Radiation in Scots Pine Pinus Sylvestris." *Trees* 27, no. 5 (June 2013): 1443–53. https://doi.org/10.1007/s00468-013-0891-z.

Müller, Christopher John. "From Radioactivity to Data Mining: Günther Anders in the Anthropocene." *Thesis Eleven* 153, no. 1 (August 2019): 9–23. https://doi.org/10.1177/0725513619867180.

Naas, Michael. "E-Phemera: Of Deconstruction, Biodegradability, and Nuclear War." In *Eco-Deconstruction: Derrida and Environmental Philosophy*, edited by Matthias Fritsch, Philippe Lynes, and David Wood, 187–205. New York: Fordham University Press, 2018.

Naas, Michael. *The End of the World and Other Teachable Moments: Jacques Derrida's Final Seminar*. New York: Fordham University Press, 2015.

Natural and Accelerated Bioremediation Research Program. *Bioremediation of Metals and Radionuclides: What It Is and How It Works*, 2nd ed. Lawrence Berkeley National Laboratory: U.S. Department of Energy, 2003.

Neyrat, Frédéric. "Ghosts of Extinction: An Essay in Spectral Ecopolitics." *The Oxford Literary Review* 41, no. 1 (July 2019): 88–106. https://doi.org/10.3366/olr.2019.0267.

Nixon, Rob. "All Tomorrow's Warnings." *Public Books*, August 13, 2020. https://www.publicbooks.org/all-tomorrows-warnings/.

Obodiac, Erin. "Introduction: Of Biodeconstruction (Part I)." *Postmodern Culture* 28, no. 3 (May 2018): [n.p.].

Obodiac, Erin, ed. "Of Biodeconstruction (Part I)." *Postmodern Culture* 28, no. 3 (May 2018).

Obodiac, Erin, ed. "Of Biodeconstruction (Part II)." *Postmodern Culture* 29, no. 1 (September 2018).

O'Connell, Mark. *Notes from an Apocalypse: A Personal Journey to the End of the World and Back*. London: Granta, 2020.

Ogilvy-Stuart, Amanda L., and Stephen M. Shalet. "Effect of Radiation on the Human Reproductive System." *Environmental Health Perspectives Supplements* 101, no. 2 (July 1993): 109–16. https://doi.org/10.2307/3431383.

Oreskes, Naomi, and Erik Conway. *The Collapse of Western Civilization: A View from the Future*. New York: Columbia University Press, 2014.

Peterson, Michael. "Responsibility and the Non(bio)degradable." In *Eco-Deconstruction: Derrida and Environmental Philosophy*, edited by Matthias Fritsch, Philippe Lynes, and David Wood, 249–60. New York: Fordham University Press, 2018.

Petter, Olivia. "Is It Monday or Wednesday? Why Lockdown Confuses Our Sense of Time." *Independent*, May 4, 2020. https://www.independent.co.uk/life-style/lockdown-time-day-week-forget-why-confused-psychology-coronavirus-a9497901.html.

Povinelli, Elizabeth A. *Geontologies: A Requiem to Late Capitalism*. Durham, NC: Duke University Press, 2016.

Pratt, Mary Louise. "Coda: Concept and Chronotope." In *Arts of Living on a Damaged Planet*, edited by Anna Tsing, Heather Swanson, Elaine Gan, and Nils Bubandt, G169–74. Minneapolis: University of Minnesota Press, 2017.

Project Persephone. http://www.projectpersephone.org/pmwiki/pmwiki.php.

Roof, Judith. *The Poetics of DNA*. Minneapolis: University of Minnesota Press, 2007.

Roosth, Sophia. "Life, Not Itself: Inanimacy and the Limits of Biology." *Grey Room* 57 (Fall 2014): 56–81. https://doi.org/10.1162/GREY_a_00156.

Roosth, Sophia. "Virus, Coal, and Seed: Subcutaneous Life in the Polar North." *Los Angeles Review of Books*, December 21, 2016. https://lareviewofbooks.org/article/virus-coal-seed-subcutaneous-life-polar-north/.

Rose, Deborah Bird. "Reflections on the Zone of the Incomplete." In *Cryopolitics: Frozen Life in a Melting World*, edited by Joanna Radin and Emma Kowal, 145–56. Cambridge, MA: MIT Press, 2017.

Runde, Wolfgang. "The Chemical Interactions of Actinides in the Environment." *Los Alamos Science* 26 (2000): 392–411.

Schuppli, Susan. "Radical Contact Prints." In *Camera Atomica*, edited by John O'Brian, 278–93. London: Black Dog, 2014.

Scranton, Roy. *Learning to Die in the Anthropocene: Reflections on the End of a Civilization*. San Francisco: City Lights Books, 2015.

Sedgwick, Adam. "Presidential Address to the Geological Society." *The Philosophical Magazine and Annals of Philosophy* 7, no. 39 (1830): 289–315.

Senatore, Mauro. *Germs of Death: The Problem of Genesis in Jacques Derrida*. Albany, NY: SUNY Press, 2018.

Sheldrake, Merlin. *Entangled Life: How Fungi Make Our Worlds, Change Our Minds, and Shape Our Futures*. London: The Bodley Head, 2020.

Smaje, Chris. "Dark Thoughts on Ecomodernism." The Dark Mountain Project, August 12, 2015. https://dark-mountain.net/dark-thoughts-on-ecomodernism-2/.

Sörlin, Sverker. "The Mirror—Testing the Counter-Anthropocene." In *Future Remains: A Cabinet of Curiosities for the Anthropocene*, edited by Gregg Mitman, Marco Armiero, and Robert S. Emmett, 169–81. Chicago: University of Chicago Press, 2018.

Subramanian, Meera. "Humans Versus Earth: The Quest to Define the Anthropocene." *Nature*, August 6, 2019. https://www.nature.com/articles/d41586-019-02381-2.

Svalbard Global Seed Vault. https://www.seedvault.no/.

Svalbard Seed Summit Press Package. "Seed Deposit 2020." Svalbard Global Seed Vault Deposit, February 25, 2020. https://www.regjeringen.no/globalassets/departementene/ud/vedlegg/nord/presskit_svalbard.pdf.

Szerszynski, Bronislaw. "The End of the End of Nature: The Anthropocene and the Fate of the Human." *The Oxford Literary Review* 34, no. 2 (December 2012): 165–84. https://doi.org/10.3366/olr.2012.0040.

Thacker, Eugene. *In the Dust of this Planet*. Winchester, UK: Zero Books, 2011.

The Frozen Ark. https://www.frozenark.org/.

Thunberg, Greta. UN Climate Change COP24 Conference. Katowice, 2018. https://www.youtube.com/watch?v=VFkQSGyeCWg&ab_channel=Connect4Climate.

Tsing, Anna Lowenhaupt. *The Mushroom at the End of the World: On the Possibility of Life in Capitalist Ruins*. Princeton, NJ: Princeton University Press, 2017.

Van Dooren, Thom. "Banking the Forest: Loss, Hope, and Care in Hawaiian Conservation." In *Cryopolitics: Frozen Life in a Melting World*, edited by Joanna Radin and Emma Kowal, 259–82. Cambridge, MA: MIT Press, 2017.

Vitale, Francesco. *Biodeconstruction: Jacques Derrida and the Life Sciences*. Translated by Mauro Senatore. Albany, NY: SUNY Press, 2018.

Vitale, Francesco. "Reading the Programme: Jacques Derrida's Deconstruction of Biology." *Postmodern Culture* 28, no. 3 (May 2018): [n.p.].

Voelz, George L. "Plutonium and Health: How Great Is the Risk?" *Los Alamos Science* 26 (2000): 74–89.

Von Verschuer, Franziska. "Freezing Lives, Preserving Humanism: Cryonics and the Promise of *Dezoefication.*" *Distinktion: Journal of Social Theory* 21, no. 2 (April 2019): 143–61. https://doi.org/10.1080/1600910X.2019.1610016.

Waters, Colin N., et al. "Can Nuclear Weapons Fallout Mark the Beginning of the Anthropocene Epoch?" *Bulletin of the Atomic Scientists* 71, no. 3 (November 2015): 46–57.

Waters, Colin N., et al. "The Anthropocene Is Functionally and Stratigraphically Distinct from the Holocene." *Science* 351, no. 6269 (January 2016): 137–47. https://doi.org/10.1126/science.aad2622.

Weisman, Alan. *The World Without Us.* London: Virgin Books, 2007.

Wills, David. *Inanimation: Theories of Inorganic Life.* Minneapolis: University of Minnesota Press, 2016.

Wollan, Malia. "Arks of the Apocalypse." *New York Times Magazine,* July 13, 2017. https://www.nytimes.com/2017/07/13/magazine/seed-vault-extinction-banks-arks-of-the-apocalypse.html.

Wood, David. *Deep Time, Dark Times: On Being Geologically Human.* New York: Fordham University Press, 2019.

Yusoff, Kathryn. *A Billion Black Anthropocenes or None.* Minneapolis: University of Minnesota Press, 2018.

Yusoff, Kathryn. "Anthropogenesis: Origins and Endings in the Anthropocene." *Theory, Culture & Society* 33, no. 2 (March 2016): 3–28. https://doi.org/10.1177/0263276415581021.

Zalasiewicz, Jan. *The Earth After Us: What Legacy Will Humans Leave in the Rocks?* Oxford: Oxford University Press, 2008.

Zalasiewicz, Jan, et al. "Are We Now Living in the Anthropocene?" *GSA Today* 18, no. 2 (February 2008): 4–8. https://doi.org/10.1130/GSAT01802A.1.

Zylinska, Joanna. *The End of Man: A Feminist Counterapocalypse.* Minneapolis: University of Minnesota Press, 2018.

Index

www.ingramcontent.com/pod-product-compliance
Lightning Source LLC
Chambersburg PA
CBHW020238290326
41929CB00044B/341